A BRIEF HISTORY

OF

THE ISLE OF MAN

Sara Goodwins

Loaghtan Books
17 Onslow Avenue
Sutton
Surrey
SM2 7ED

Published by Loaghtan Books

First published: April 2011

Copyright © Sara Goodwins, 2011

Typesetting and origination by:
Loaghtan Books

Printed and bound by:
Gomer Press Limited

Website: www.loaghtanbooks.com

ISBN: 978 1 908060 00 6

Photographic copyright © George Hobbs 2011

For David Ashworth,
whose idea this book was in the first place,
and without whose patience and advice
it would not have been published.

Front cover: Viking ship burial, Balladoole near Castletown. The stones are not original but placed to mark where the ship rested

Rear cover: The cottages at Niarbyl. The name comes from the Manx *yn arbyl* which means the tail. Opposite the cottages is a line of rocks stretching out to sea. Perhaps they're trying to reach America to which they were once joined.

Title page: The Calf of Man cross reproduced in the stained glass window of Cregneash church. The design dates from the ninth century, the church from the nineteenth and the window from the twentieth

CONTENTS

1   The Dawn of Time   5

2   Bronze Age, Iron Age and why the Romans never came to Mann   15

3   Invaders from the North   27

4   The Scots, the English and the Lords of Mann   46

5   Two and a half centuries of Stanleys   61

6   The Stanleys rise again   79

7   The English, Emigration and Entrepreneurs   92

8   Changing Emphasis   113

9   Selected Myths and Mysteries; the Alternative History   131

Appendices

1   Kings and things   142

2   Bishops of Sodor and Man   145

3   The Tynwald Ceremony   147

    Selected Bibliography   148

    Brief Index   150

THE ISLE OF MAN

The sketch map below is intended only to give a rough idea of the location of some of the places mentioned in the text. Those travelling by car would be advised to use the 1:50,000 Ordnance Survey (OS) Landranger Map, sheet 95 (the pink one). Walkers should use either the OS map or the 1:25,000 Public Rights of Way and Outdoor Leisure Map published by the Isle of Man Government.

CHAPTER 1

THE DAWN OF TIME

If you stand on the summit of Snaefell on a clear day you can see seven kingdoms, or so the story goes: Mann (of course), England, Wales, Scotland, Ireland, the ocean, which is Neptune's Kingdom and heaven, the Kingdom of God. From Snaefell you can see the great panorama of neighbouring islands circling around Mann in the centre, like the rim of a tea cup circling the bubbles in the middle. If the light is right – and it doesn't happen often – the islands of Britain seem close enough for you to reach out your hand and pluck Scafell Pike from the Lake District or cradle the Mountains of Mourne in the palm of your hand.

The creation of an island

What people don't think about when admiring the fabulous view is that Mann and its neighbouring islands are all joined together under the sea. The Isle of Man, the rest of Britain, Ireland and most of continental Europe are part of what is now the Eurasian plate, one piece of the jigsaw of tectonic plates which make up the Earth's outer layer or crust. The tectonic plates float on the semi-molten rock which makes up the earth's mantle. Because they float they bump against each other, albeit very slowly, causing earthquakes and volcanoes and creating new earth formations. The Eurasian plate also includes Russia and China and half of Iceland. The other half of Iceland is part of the North American plate. The two plates are gradually drifting apart, Europe is retreating from North America and the centre of Iceland is sinking.

Rock formations at Marine Drive. The layers are the sandstone and mudstone beds of the Manx Group. They were horizontal before tilting and folding when Avalonia and Laurentia collided

That's the situation now, but 500 million years ago things, as you would expect, were very different.   The Isle of Man is now on latitude 55 degrees north but was then thousands of miles to the south on latitude 60 degrees south, between where Cape Horn and Antarctica is today. It was part of a small landmass called Avalonia which also included what was to become England, Wales and the south and east of Ireland. Scotland and the north and west of Ireland were part of a continent called Laurentia which also included North America and Greenland. Avalonia and Laurentia were separated by the Iapetus Ocean which was roughly as wide as the Atlantic between Newfoundland and Ireland today.

Over the next 90 million years the bed of the Iapetus Ocean was covered with layer upon layer of sediment which gradually hardened to form what is known as the Manx Group of rocks. During these millennia the two continents Avalonia and Laurentia were also drifting together. They eventually collided about 410 million years ago, crumpled at the edges and formed the Caledonian Mountain range which probably equalled the size of the Himalayas today. The collision of the two continental plates brought together the northern and southern parts of the British Isles.

Ruins of St Peter's Church, Peel. Built of Peel sandstone, which is soft, the details erode quickly

At this time, about 400 million years ago, the Isle of Man together with the rest of the British Isles lay south of the equator and the huge mountain range was subject to heat, wind and seasonal rainfall. As the mountains eroded, rivers moved large quantities of sand and pebbles and dumped them in low-lying areas where the wind evaporated the surface water and blew the sand into dunes. Over time the distinctive dark red sand compressed into rocks and became what is now known as Peel Sandstone. Sandstone is a freestone, which means that it can be cut in any direction. Peel Sandstone is the only freestone on Mann and was often used in buildings. It is however very soft and erodes easily so modern buildings tend to be built of a less friable stone of similar colour which has been imported.

The rock formations which were to become the Isle of Man continued to drift northwards until, around 330 million years ago, they reached the equator. Warm shallow tropical seas teeming with marine life covered most of what would become Mann. Shells are made out of calcium carbonate and it is layers of the ancient shells which form the carboniferous limestone now found around Castletown and Port St Mary. Limestone is particularly hard wearing and much of the old part of Castletown, including Castle Rushen and Langness lighthouse, was built using the local stone. A particularly good example of the use of local limestone is Scarlett House built of stone from the nearby Scarlett quarry. A dark coloured variation of the limestone nicknamed 'black marble' was quarried a mile or so northwest at Poyllvaaish and used for various decorative purposes. Cemeteries on the island have tombstones made of the Poyllvaaish black marble and the quarry was reopened to produce monumental crosses to commemorate the second calendar millennium.

Millions more years passed and the land which was to become the Isle of Man continued its progress northwards. Relatively little changed its essential composition until it reached its present location. The world had gradually been getting colder and about two million years ago experienced the start of the Ice Age. Huge glaciers spread down from the arctic covering most of Britain with sheet ice. The ice advanced and retreated several times, sometimes covering

Example of millennium commemorative stone. The style is the same, each stone differing only in the name. Fairly obviously, this one is at Ballaugh

the whole of what was to become Mann, sometimes covering only part of it. The ice scoured out valleys, rounded off hills and dumped rock debris as the ice melted. The northern end of the island, the northern plain, is formed entirely from glacial deposits. Such deposits are soft and, as the ice moved southwards. it pushed the soft debris in front of it rather like pushing wrinkles in soft cloth and created what are called moraine ridges. The hills around Bride are what remains of glacial moraine and show the southern limits of the last glacier to reach Mann.

After the glaciers finally withdrew, Mann, not yet an island, would first have been bare of vegetation or animal life. Quickly, small plants, similar to the arctic plants of today, would have colonised the bare ground and grazing animals would have taken advantage of them.

Palaeolithic or Early Stone Age people were nomads, following the best sources of food, whether that was ripening plants, or herds which they could hunt for food. They lived in small skin shelters and followed the animals they hunted, but no record is left of their presence on the island. Glaciers obliterate entire landscapes, never mind the fugitive remnants of nomadic families with no settled home. As the animals sought the best grazing, so they would have been followed by nomadic people. The first people to make Mann their base could well have walked here.

Langness Lighthouse. Completed in 1880, it was built using durable local limestone

The First Manxman

It was the Ice Age which turned Mann into an island. About 15,000 years ago the climate became warmer and the ice sheet melted. The sea level rose and gradually flooded the valleys between what was left of the peaks of the Caledonian Mountain range. The land link between the Isle of Man and Ireland ended about 12,000 years ago; that between the Isle of Man and the UK about 2,000 years later.

At the beginning of the Mesolithic period or Middle Stone Age, mammoths, hippos, giant deer and great bears had inhabited large parts of what became the British Isles, but something happened to make the very large animals die out. Some of the last of the giant deer seem to have survived for centuries longer on the Isle of Man, possibly protected by the lack of human hunters on the island and outliving their contemporaries in what was to become continental Europe. Giant deer were thought to have been extinct by 8,000 BC, but an almost complete skeleton of one was found at Ballaugh in 1815 which has been dated to about 7,000 BC. That skeleton was given to the Edinburgh museum, but a particularly good example found at Close y Garey in 1887 is on display at the Manx Museum. Probably because of their huge antlers, giant deer are occasionally known as Irish Elk. The title is inaccurate however as the animal is neither Irish nor an elk. Its nearest modern relative is the fallow deer.

Ballaglass Glen. 9,000 years ago, this type of mixed woodland covered most of the Manx upland

As the climate grew warmer the cold tundra which had been the character of the land after the ice receded began to give way to trees. Mixed deciduous woodland, not unlike that which now colonises the Manx national glens, would have spread over much of the island, with pine and birch trees on many of the uplands. The first people to live on the Isle of Man would have been hunter-gatherers like their Palaeolithic predecessors and appeared around 7,000 BC. Why they came to the Isle of Man we don't know but the immigration would not have been undertaken lightly. The only boats of the time were dug-out canoes and possibly portable hide boats similar to coracles, useful for a nomadic lifestyle along the coast. Whatever the reason for coming to Mann, the island obviously had suitable or even desirable living conditions for people as they stayed.

The new Manx people lived a nomadic lifestyle in extended family groups with more gathering than hunting. Certainly they ate meat and fish, but most of their diet consisted of roots, leaves, berries, nuts, insects, eggs and shellfish. Anyone who has ever been camping will know that, once the tent has been removed there is remarkably little left to show any details about who was living there and how, so traces of Mesolithic people are extremely fugitive. The

Snaefell summit was part of the Caledonian Mountain range which continues today through Scotland. This view looks north west along the spine of hills to North Barrule. Ramsey is just visible on the coast

most obvious permanent traces which hunter-gatherers leave behind them is evidence of flint working and it is this evidence which has been found for example in the south of the island at Billown and under Ronaldsway airport. Judging by such remnants the incomers probably came from Ireland as the remains found of their flint tools are remarkably similar to those used in Northern Ireland at the time.

Mesolithic people expanded their range of tools as their skill at working flint became more sophisticated. Instead of shaping a single piece of flint into whatever tool the flint knapper wanted, it gradually became the norm to use a combination of materials to produce different tools. Stone axes were developed during the Middle Stone Age, usually with a flint blade inserted through a wooden handle and bound in place with leather thongs, plant fibres, or animal sinews. The habit of combining materials into more efficient tools is most obvious in the development of microliths. Microliths are triangular pieces of flint about the size of a fingernail and were inset into antler or bone handles to make a variety of different tools either with sharp points, such as spears, harpoons and arrows, or with barbed cutting edges such as knives or something which resembled a sickle or small scythe.

Despite the development of all this new technology, communities were still nomadic with people following animal herds or moving to take advantage of plants in season. Everything the communities owned would have been light and portable. Clothes and shelters were made from animal hide, tools from horn, bone or flint, baskets were woven from reeds, grasses or supple twigs, rope was twisted from animal gut or creeping plants such as honeysuckle, needles were fashioned from antler or fish bone.

The Mesolithic period lasted from around 9,000 BC to 4,000 BC during which people slowly evolved from being 'pure' hunters to something part-way between hunter and farmer. Over a period of time, hunter-gatherers generally favoured one site over others, possibly because of some natural shelter, access to clean water, an abundant supply of plant food or good hunting grounds. They would still have left their favoured site for periods of time as the seasons changed, but would probably have returned to it as a semi-permanent home.

Living on an island the Manx would not have been able to cover the huge distances travelled by continental hunter-gatherers and would probably have relied much more on a diet of fish and seaweed. An island race would naturally take to fishing but frequent travel across the sea would have been risky and possibly viewed as unnecessary. There was probably regular contact with tribes in Ireland and Scotland however, in view of the similarity of tools. As many of the foodstuffs of Mann's indigenous people would have been concentrated into a relatively small area they may even have been one of the earlier people to adopt a more permanent way of life. Such a suggestion has some backing from recent research which has found that permanent

Manx loaghtan. A modern survivor thought to bear a close resemblance to prehistoric sheep

settlements began to be created in Ireland and Scotland – the neighbours with whom the Manx people had the most contact – during the Neolithic period but that England and Wales had to wait until the Bronze Age for the creation of settled communities.

From foraging to farming

Of course hunter-gatherers didn't wake up one morning and decide that they would be farmers from now on. The Neolithic or New Stone Age lasted from about 4,000 to about 2,500 BC and it was during these two thousand years that people began to create the first permanent settlements and adapt to a different way of living. Communities began growing their own food and domesticating animals, rather than relying on what they could find in season and/or hunt. Again the question is why the change, and again we don't really know. One of the arguments put forward is that the population was increasing and the land could no longer support the lifestyle of a hunter-gatherer. If more people needed to be fed, then more food was required, and this meant either improving gathering techniques or deliberately encouraging and planting the right sort of plants to produce a bigger harvest. The argument would definitely make sense for an island race where a nomadic life was of necessity confined to a relatively small area and where the amount of dependable food gathered from the land is more obviously finite.

In a settled lifestyle the emphasis changed from things needing to be light enough to carry, to being strong enough to withstand bad weather without needing constant repair. Rather than structures being made of flexible poles and skins they began to be built of heavier timber and stone with turf or thatched roofs. The same is true of boats of the time. Canoes dating from the Neolithic period have been found on the island; the most complete example was discovered at

Ballakaighan in 1884 and closely resembled canoes of a similar age found near the Clyde. The canoe is heavy and although certainly portable not easy to carry for any distance.

With farming producing a crop larger than required for immediate use people began to store the surplus against future famine. Simple ploughs called ards, hauled and steered by people, were first used during the Neolithic period and made possible the cultivation of larger areas of land. Communities also minimised the unpredictability of relying on hunting and began to keep within a restricted area those animals they wanted for meat, milk, hide, wool, etc.

Sheep were known to be first domesticated during the New Stone Age and would have been similar in appearance to the Manx Loaghtan. The name, which is sometimes spelt Loaghtyn or Loghtan, is believed to come from the Manx words *lugh* (mouse) and *dhone* (brown) and probably refers to the attractive colour of the fleece and the animals' size. The sheep are small, hardy, lack wool on their legs and face and have four or occasionally six horns. The Loaghtan, together with breeds such as the Soay which are native to other islands, are the nearest modern equivalent of prehistoric sheep.

A stationary lifestyle such as was developed during the Neolithic also made the use of pottery practical for the first time. Pots are time-consuming to make and too fragile to be of much use to people constantly on the move, but have obvious advantages once the need for safe transportation has passed. Neolithic pots were made by coiling long strips of clay in a rising spiral, smoothing over the sides and hardening the result in a hot, controlled fire. People had been using fire for thousands of years but it was during the New Stone Age that they learned some of the sophistications needed to control its temperature. It is probable that Neolithic pots were hardened in an early form of kiln called a clamp, where combustible material is stacked around the newly-made pots, and its burning is controlled under turf to retain the heat. Early Neolithic pots had no decoration, but later ones had designs marked on the clay such as scratched herringbone patterns, finger prints, or the impression of grains of wheat.

One Neolithic settlement containing pottery fragments and some large pottery jars was found at Ronaldsway where the remains of a New Stone Age dwelling was discovered when the airport was being

Cashtel-yn-Ard. The most complete Neolithic site on the Isle of Man

built in 1943. The Ronaldsway culture shows distinctions thought to be unique to the Isle of Man, not least in some of its pottery. The jars are fairly crude, about 20ins tall and about 11ins in diameter with thick, straight-sided walls and round bases. Similar pots have been found at other sites throughout the island, including four at Billown in 1996.

Tools were always very important and, as with pottery, the Isle of Man can claim a unique Ronaldsway variation. Flint scrapers were used throughout the Stone Age to clean animal skins of fat and meat before curing. They were shaped a little like a modern comb, with the scraper part replacing the comb's teeth. Neolithic examples found on the Isle of Man show a unique variation however. Known as 'hump-backed' scrapers, one side of the back of the scraper rises into a lump or hump. Scrapers of this shape appear to exist partly because the raw material from which the scraper was fashioned was a rounded pebble, but also because the 'hump' fits neatly into the palm of the hand making the scraper easier to hold and use.

The most unusual finds dating from Stone Age Ronaldsway are five oval slate plaques about 3ins long and 1½ ins wide. Two of the plaques are decorated with chevrons incised into the surface and all are smoothed and polished. The trouble is that we don't know what they are! It is possible that they were simply ornaments, had a ceremonial significance, were trading items or possibly even counters in some kind of early game, although the care taken over their preparation makes this latter perhaps less likely. A similar plaque has been found at Ballavarry as well as plaque fragments in Onchan.

The gradual development of permanent settlements means that the detritus of ordinary living was not only concentrated in one area, but also made of more durable material. People of the New Stone Age became builders, not only of domestic accommodation, but also, apparently for the first time, of permanent structures with ceremonial significance. It is the structures concerned with the supernatural, the afterlife, and the rituals which served both which survive best, rather as cathedrals survive better than humble cottages today.

Ballafayle Cairn. A Neolithic site just south of Ballajora, excavated by Manx antiquities expert, P.M.C. Kermode

A Brief History of the Isle of Man

Dealing with the Dead

Most of the ceremonial structures found on Mann tend to be similar to those found on Neolithic sites in other countries. Religion tends to be conservative; the way of life of people of the same religion may differ often quite radically, but their religious rites, observances and buildings tend to be much more similar. Even so, at least one of the Manx ceremonial sites is unusual and perhaps unique.

The Isle of Man has several well-preserved Neolithic sites, the most complete of which is Cashtal yn Ard. Dating from about 2,000 BC Cashtal yn Ard, when complete, was at least 130 ft long and forty-five wide. It's a long oval with a forecourt at the west end marked by a semicircle of eight standing stones radiating out like horns, and is one of the largest of this type of barrow in the British Isles.

Originally surmounted by a great cairn stone covered with earth, only the stone skeleton of the barrow now remains, revealing the grave gallery of five compartments separated by upright slabs. Excavations have revealed flint, pottery and human bones, including part of a skull and upper jaw bone. This type of cairn was often used as a depository for cremated remains for hundreds and

Meayll Circle. A possibly unique circular arrangement of burial chambers

occasionally thousands of years. The entrance to the burial chamber was from the west and facing the setting sun, but the original approach was from the east. The symbolism is therefore of life approaching death. The footpath to Cashtal-yn-Ard still approaches from the east and visitors must tread a path used for over four millennia.

Neolithic burial sites are usually on high ground and often visible from some distance away; Cashtal-yn-Ard commands a superb 360-degree view. Archaeologists surmise that the monuments act as a reminder of the tribe's ancestors, are at a point where earth and sky meet so mark a meeting place between this world and the next, and possibly act as a beacon to neighbouring tribes – an announcement that 'we are here, this is our place'. Whatever the reason Cashtal-yn-Ard has company. Another Neolithic burial, Ballafayle Cairn, of a slightly later date tops a neighbouring hill to the north east. Whether the two were in use at similar times by different tribes, one took precedence over the other or they were used in series we can't be sure.

Ballafayle Cairn lies almost within line of sight of Cashtal-yn-Ard; certainly the trees which are near both sites can be seen from each. Maps sometimes refer to Ballafayle Cairn as the Short Horned Cairn, but this is nothing to do with cattle. It refers rather to the cairn's crescent-shaped façade which probably included short projecting wings bounding a forecourt. When the cairn was partially excavated in 1926 there was evidence of prolonged burning and human cremation. A number of white shore pebbles of various sizes were found at the cairn, including a large one on the clay floor close to the cremated bones. Such shore pebbles are present in other Neolithic burials, including those at Mull Hill near Cregneash. It seems that they may have been used for some ritual purpose, although what that was we can only guess.

The Mull Hill chambered tomb known as the Meayll Circle is the Isle of Man's unusual and possibly unique Neolithic burial site. Often marked on old maps as a stone circle it is in fact a ring of six pairs of burial chambers arranged in two sets of three with a gap at each end facing roughly north west and south east; the northern entrance faces Bradda Head and the sea. Series of paired burial chambers with gaps between them are known elsewhere, but the tombs at the top of Mull Hill appear to be unique in that the burial chambers are arranged in a circle. Each pair takes the form of a T with the downstroke of the letter facing away from the centre of the circle. The downstroke acts as a passageway to the two burial chambers on either side and each T appears to be roughly paved. Apart from flint arrow heads, scrapers and knives plus the remains of at least twenty-six different burial urns many of which contained evidence of cremated human bones, the Meayll Circle is particularly noted for yielding Neolithic pottery of the Ronaldsway type.

And the afterlife?
The permanence of burial sites and the way they were looked after suggests that Neolithic people respected their dead and had a growing reverence for the supernatural. It's during the late Neolithic that people first started building henge monuments. Henges are generally accepted to be sites of ritual activity possibly linked with a greater understanding of both the natural and supernatural worlds. A henge is like an inside-out fort. Like a fort it's usually a circle of ditches and banks sometimes with a stone or wooden structure in the middle. Unlike a fort the ditches are on the inside of the bank circle rather than the outside and so are of little use for defence in the traditional sense – although it has been suggested that rather than being built to protect those inside from what was happening outside, they were built to protect those outside from whatever was going on inside.

Most people think of henge monuments as being very large. Avebury in England, the Ring of Brodgar in Scotland or Rath Maeve in Ireland are all huge for example, but henges don't have to be big. It is use and appearance rather than size which denotes a henge. Current archaeological work in Billown has discovered what is possibly a mini henge about 10 ft across. Building a henge was a considerable undertaking. Even a small one would have taken days, possibly weeks of work. They also required great social co-operation. Henge builders needed to be supported by their community and their existence argues that their society had an abundance of food and natural resources to be able to spare people for the work. The needs of the builders not only had to be met by the work of their peers, it also deprived the tribe of whatever contribution the henge builders might otherwise have been making. Henges started to appear in the late Neolithic but really developed during a period of history which had huge significance for the Isle of Man. The Bronze Age.

CHAPTER 2

BRONZE AGE, IRON AGE AND WHY THE ROMANS NEVER CAME TO MANN

Although the Bronze Age can be dated as starting from around 2,500 BC when people first began to use bronze implements, the Neolithic lifestyle lasted relatively unchanged for several centuries. In fact the use of stone never completely died out during the Bronze Age, probably because stone, unlike bronze, was usually available locally. Nevertheless as stone tools were gradually superseded by bronze equivalents less care was taken in their manufacture and far less status given to their use.

As an island people the Manx would of course have used boats and been familiar with their building and it is during the Bronze Age that truly sea-going vessels began to be developed. Bronze Age boats were about 30 ft long and about 8 ft wide, flat bottomed but with a steep upward curve at the sides and at either end. Those few which survive are made of thick oak planks sewn together with yew withies and are both strong and very flexible. The joins are sealed with moss and clay, and the seal then covered with oak laths. Each vessel could carry probably about five tons of cargo, although historians are not sure whether such boats were paddled or sailed – oars were not known in Northern Europe at that time.

Jarlshof, Shetland. One of the best preserved late Bronze Age/early Iron Age communities. The remains of several such communities have been found on Mann, although none are so well preserved

Sea-going vessels meant easier and more frequent contact with people on the neighbouring islands, particularly as the Isle of Man would have been a convenient stopping point for ships travelling across the Irish Sea. The Manx would therefore have been influenced by differing lifestyles as different groups of seafarers sheltered in the island's natural harbours. One group, often called the beaker folk from their style of pottery, originated in central Europe. Their customs and skills gradually began to influence communities around them and before long spread to the British Isles including the Isle of Man.

Bronze provides an edge

Bronze is an alloy made of about nine parts copper to one part tin, although lead was added to the mix later in the Bronze Age to make the alloy easier to pour into moulds. The Isle of Man was rich in lead and had copper deposits at Bradda and Langness, but tin is relatively rare.

The only two sources of tin in Europe are south-west Britain, particularly Cornwall, and Spain. Copper waste was found with other scrap at Ballagawne, not far from Port St Mary, and part of a sandstone mould into which molten metal would have been poured was discovered at Kiondroughad, Andreas. Some metalworking was therefore undertaken in Mann in the first millennium BC and trade must have supplied the necessary tin.

Close ny Chollagh, near Scarlett. Little remains to be seen of the round houses; the earthworks are the remnants of a promontory fort

Ireland was a major producer of bronze items, having good supplies of copper and regular access to English tin. The Isle of Man had had trading and cultural links with Ireland since Neolithic times and many of the Bronze Age implements discovered on Mann show a marked resemblance to those found in Ireland from a similar period. Knives and axes were the earliest bronze implements to be made and were at first very scarce. They were almost always for display and ceremonial use, with stone tools continuing to be used for day-to-day tasks. Most of the Bronze Age implements which survive were given as grave goods, i.e. buried with a corpse or cremated remains, so their design and quality are not necessarily typical of items intended for regular use.

Chysauster, Cornwall, England. The Close ny Chollach community may have lived in houses something like this

Community life

During the Bronze Age the building of massive burial monuments which were a feature of the Neolithic gradually gave way to the construction and use of smaller barrows, each often still containing more than one burial. In the early Bronze Age people were buried curled into a foetal position on their side; the Bronze Age burial at Killeaba, Ramsey, for example, contained four crouch burials of three adults and a child. Over the next thousand years or so customs changed and cremation became the

A Brief History of the Isle of Man

norm, with the cremated bones interred in large urns. If the outward signs of burial were more modest, the grave goods were not, and axes, bangles, pots and weaponry have all been founded buried with their owners or as offerings made to gods or ancestors.

Bronze Age barrows still form distinctive features in the landscape; there have been suggestions that even Tynwald Hill may originally have been a Bronze Age burial mound, as such barrows occasionally formed local assembly places. Bronze Age barrows with their central burial are surprisingly similar in design to Bronze Age round houses with their central hearth. The similarity of form might have been a deliberate attempt to link dwellings in this world with a life in the next.

It was during the Bronze Age that the landscape of the island began to take on a form which would be familiar today. The different communities or tribes needed to communicate with each other and their fields, so primitive roads and trackways became much more a feature of the landscape. Trees were cleared and fields and paddocks laid out, separated from each other by drystone walls or possibly the sod hedges typical of Mann. Sod hedges are built of soil and turf and designed as a barrier for livestock. They're usually about six feet high and six broad made from turf cut from land on either side of the hedge to make a ditch. The turf is laid like bricks to make two outer walls before the core is filled with stone and compacted soil. A sod hedge can also be added to the top of an existing wall or a wall built first and a sod hedge added. Various plants, herbs and even trees such as hawthorn or gorse can then either grow naturally or be grown on top of the hedge the whole providing a sturdy windbreak and attractive barrier.

Bronze Age Beaker. A commemorative stamp from 1976 showing a beaker found in Barroose, just west of Baldrine

The population of the Isle of Man grew during the Bronze Age and people lived in settled communities mainly concentrated on farming, but regularly supplementing their diet with fishing and hunting. Round houses had low stone or timber walls supporting a conical roof of turf or thatch and were frequently shared by an extended family and their animals. As a result they were often very large, with a floor area at least twice that of the average family home today. The hearth was in the middle of the house and there was no chimney, so smoke found its way out through the roof as it could. This was not as daft as it sounds. Dry wood can burn with little smoke and a chimney creates a through draft, introducing more oxygen and so causing a fire to burn more fiercely. From their smelting work, Bronze Age people would understand how to manage fire. They may well have chosen not to build a funnel chimney in order to avoid a fiercely-burning fire beneath a large roof of highly combustible material. In any case, the climate at the time is generally thought to have been warmer so fires in the round houses may have been more important for cooking than heating.

One of the most extensive collection of round houses on Mann is north and east of the Meayll Circle on Mull Hill. The circle itself was built during the Neolithic (see Chapter 1) but the area continued in use well into the Bronze Age and possibly beyond. A few of the round houses even appeared to be semi-detached, with walls adjoining neighbouring dwellings. They were built in a hollow, presumably to shelter them from wind and weather, with their entrances facing north. By the late Bronze Age, farmsteads were usually made up of clusters of several roundhouses. Most of the animals still farmed today were domesticated by this time, so farms could have contained cattle, pigs, sheep, poultry, goats, horses and dogs, although in varying numbers depending on the suitability of the land. Clothing was probably a mix of hide and woven material.

Bronze Age round houses were often used for centuries, presumably passed on through families. Three found at Ballakaighen, north and slightly west of Castletown, were probably inhabited into the Iron Age. They were around 90ft in diameter with turf-covered timber roofs supported by oak posts. Over the years some 4,000 (yes, 4,000) mature oak trees had been felled to build and maintain the dwelling which would have been home to many generations.

An extended family meant a lot of mouths to feed and mounds excavated at Clay Head, just south of Garwick, proved to be an open-air cooking site; a sort of Bronze Age barbeque. The mounds themselves were made of waste from cooking stones which had eventually shattered after much use. Bronze Age pottery wouldn't stand direct contact with fire so liquids had to be warmed indirectly. Stones were heated in a fire, removed using tongs made out of the forked branch of a tree, plunged quickly into washing water to remove ash and cinders and then dropped, still very hot, into liquid to heat it. The method is surprisingly quick and efficient. An area the size of Clay Head, used from around 2,200 to 1,050 BC, suggests more than domestic cooking however and could have been a feasting place for communities, even perhaps an area where people from different tribes could meet in peace.

Us and them

One consequence of the growth of permanent settlements and an increasing population is that competition for food and natural resources also increased. There would have been more jockeying for position while the investment of time, effort and resources in building and farming, would have meant a distinct unwillingness to move unless absolutely essential. Local inhabitants probably had trading and marital ties with folk from the neighbouring islands, and ideas as well as trade goods crossed the water. The idea that where you lived made a difference to who you were, or that different countries encapsulated and defined different races, was still in its infancy. Communities were based around the tribe, which might well have its own laws and customs. Disputes must have occurred before the Bronze Age, but any fighting had been conducted either with fists or using tools which were principally designed for hunting and domestic use – spears, knives and axes. Only during the Bronze Age did implements begin to be made which had no other purpose than conflict. For the first time people began to make swords.

The summit of South Barrule. A large hill fort with inner and outer rampart still visible, South Barrule is the largest hill fort on Mann

Bronze Age swords are often described as leaf-shaped, although this would be aspidistra rather than oak. Above the hilt the narrow waist widened out into a fairly broad blade – broad for a sword that is – before tapering again to a point. A virtually complete

A Brief History of the Isle of Man

South Barrule is the highest mountain in the south of the island so those living here would have been able to see invaders not just from Mann, but also from the surrounding islands

sword was found at Berrag, north east of Sandygate, and can be seen in the Manx Museum.

With an increase in the importance placed on land and property came an increase in disagreements, and with an increase in disagreements came the need to defend and fortify. The existence of a fort does not immediately imply warfare, but it does suggest that people felt less secure. The summit of South Barrule is circled by the double rampart of a late Bronze Age or early Iron Age fort. Partial excavation in 1960-1 has shown that the inner rampart was also protected by sharpened stakes embedded at an angle; the turf-backed stone bracing for the base of the stakes still remains. The outer rampart lacks such protection but was more solidly built with a vertical dry-stone face on the outside. It encloses an area roughly 600 ft in diameter, making it the largest as well as the highest hill fort on the island.

The word 'fort' can be misunderstood. Certainly the huge structures were intended partly for defence but were also meant to deter by their impressive size and bulk. There were simply not enough people willing to co-operate in waging large pitched battles and most fighting between tribes would have been in the nature of raids on cattle, land and stores. There are around 3,500 Iron Age hill forts in Britain, over twenty of which are on Mann. Each constituted a huge expenditure of effort, but the statement of intent must have been worth it to protect the tribe's possessions.

South Barrule from Snaefell

Within the fort on South Barrule are traces of over seventy round stone-walled huts. From about 200 BC people seemed to gather together in greater numbers and such a large collection of round houses possibly indicates an embryo town.

Going Grey

The beginning of the Iron Age marked much more than exchanging brown metal for grey. According to the pollen record, the climate appears to have grown colder, which probably meant that natural resources were scarcer and people had to work harder to survive. The advent of hill forts indicates that competition between families and tribes may have intensified. Society also appears to have grown more hierarchical as such competition seems to have been spearheaded by powerful leaders. Rather than sharing burial sites, which were more common in the Neolithic and Bronze Ages, burials from the Iron Age are more often of high-status individuals who are interred with a range of quality grave goods.

Although iron was more difficult to work than bronze, it was also much harder and therefore more useful. Any cutting utensil needs a durable edge and iron made much better blades for knives, sickles, axes and swords. The metal was probably first introduced to Mann as traded ingots, but the island is rich in iron ore, with surface deposits at Maughold, so the Manx people must have started exploiting their own mineral resources quite soon. Excavations at several Iron Age sites around the island have revealed moulds, finishing tools, ore and slag.

Despite the evidence of early industry the Iron Age way of life was still largely agricultural with farmers raising sheep, cattle and pigs, and growing peas, beans and wheat. Grain for eating would probably have been stored in granaries raised off the ground while grain for planting was often stored in underground pits sealed with clay. The top layer of grain sprouted, used up the available oxygen and stopped growing. Without oxygen the storage pit was sterile as long as it remained sealed.

In Ireland at this time families had what would today be considered an odd arrangement when it came to child rearing. After the age of about seven, children were often placed with foster parents rather than raised within their own family. There were two sorts of fosterage; fostering for affection and fostering for payment. The idea was to strengthen family connexions and ensure that children learned skills which their own parents might lack. Fosterage also tended to make society more peaceable; your neighbour would be less likely to attack you or steal your cattle if you were raising his heir. Girls stayed in fosterage until they reached fourteen, boys until seventeen – think of it as similar to a boarding school today. Some form of fostering was certainly known on Mann, as the Mal Lumkun cross in Kirk Michael shows.

The Mal Lumkun cross in Kirk Michael. The runes on the back say: 'Mal Lumkun erected this cross in memory of Mal Mura his foster [mother]... Better it is to leave a good foster son than a bad son'

A Brief History of the Isle of Man

Iron Age families lived in round houses similar to Bronze Age dwellings and, as well as the means for domestic metalworking, each house would almost certainly have contained one or more looms for weaving cloth; archaeologists regularly find loom weights when excavating Iron Age round houses. Little pottery is found on Mann from this time. Drinking and cooking vessels may have been made of wood or horn while storage containers were probably various forms of baskets or made of wood or hide. One unusual domestic find on Mann dates from around 450BC and is possibly the earliest human flea found in Britain! It was found beneath a buried wooden post from what had been a farming community on St Patrick's Isle.

Four Iron Age round houses, two of them well preserved, were excavated at Close ny Chollagh, west of Castletown, in 1953-6. They had square central hearths, paved entrances and elaborate drainage which makes them very similar to the houses in the Iron Age villages of Chysauster and Carn Euny in Cornwall. In the houses were found a semi-circular bone comb with twelve teeth, and a fibula brooch, i.e. one with a bar front and which fastens with a simple pin, like those on some modern badges. The brooch dates to around 80 BC and shows that the houses were still in use at that time.

Even more impressive are the three pale green glass beads which were excavated in 1985 from the site of an Iron Age dwelling at Braust, just west of the disused airfield near Andreas. Iron Age glass is extremely rare and very few glass beads have been discovered in Britain. Most glass was made in continental Europe at this time, particularly in what is now northern France, and it has been suggested that glass beads were valuable trading items, acting as a kind of rudimentary currency. Coins first appeared in England and Wales during the middle Iron Age but weren't in use in Scotland and don't appear to have been acceptable on Mann as none has been found.

The usual form for Iron Age glass beads is a hoop or ring through which a cord can be passed. This arrangement would have been useful either when worn as decoration or for carrying as trading tokens. The Manx beads are very unusual as they are shaped something like dumbbells or the buttons on a modern duffle coat. Each would have been worn hung from a cord secured by a knot tied round the thinner shank in the middle of the bead. They are very high status items and their unusual design possibly indicates local manufacture.

Escape from Rome

Most people know that the Romans never conquered Mann but this doesn't mean that the island was totally unaffected by the Empire looming just across the water. It also doesn't mean that Roman traders never came here. As is the case with most conquerors, the Romans were superbly indifferent to the geography of countries lying outside the borders of the Empire. Julius Caesar, Pliny the Elder and Ptolemy all knew of Mann, sometimes called it Mona but more usually Monapia, and often got its location wildly wrong. Confusingly, 'Mona's Isle', which today must mean the Isle of Man, could for the Romans also mean the Isle of Anglesey off the north-west coast of Wales.

Not only did the classical world know about Mann, Roman galleys patrolled the western coast of England and Wales and Roman merchantmen ventured to Ireland, so may even have stopped at a Manx port. In general Roman civilisation took no account of the sea, while Roman people considered sailors to be second-class citizens. Their navy was considered inferior to their army and under the latter's control. Not only did the Romans dislike the sea they also loathed Britain. They considered the province cold, wet, infested by dangerous barbarians and only tolerable because of its mineral wealth. It's likely therefore that the Romans would have been condescending towards those living on a small island even further north and west than the hated ends of empire. However it also seems most unlikely that the skilled Manx seafarers didn't try to profit from any lucrative Roman trade conducted under their noses, whether that profit was legitimate or not.

The Romans used the term 'pirate' at sea much as they used the word 'barbarian' on land. To Romans a pirate was any sailor in their waters who was not Roman; Manx sailors would therefore all have been pirates and subject to Roman piracy law if caught. And Romans took the threat seriously. On Holyhead island on the Isle of Anglesey beyond the north west coast of Wales is a heavily fortified signal tower at Caer Y Twr which might also have been a Pharos or early lighthouse. It commands a view west over the Irish Sea and was built to provide early warnings against Irish raiders. Mann's links with Iron Age Ireland are obvious. Many of the Manx churches are dedicated to Celtic Irish saints. Irish decoration and inscriptions are relatively common and Irish sources at the time suggest that the Irish considered Mann as belonging to Ireland. Below Caer y Twr in Holyhead itself are the remains of a small Roman fort, built to protect the harbour against such raiders. It's unlikely that, when raiders came from the sea, the Romans would have stopped to enquire whether they were Irish or Manx.

Spooyt Vane, Glen Mooar. The impressive waterfall with its pool was traditionally the site of Druidical worship

Advent of Christianity

The Iron Age first saw Christianity come to Mann. Pre-Christian religion on the island was probably Druidical, although Druids also had a semi-political role as law-givers and advisors. Within Celtic society they sanctioned war, acted as keepers of knowledge, judged disputes, and supervised sacrifices and religious ceremonies. Certainly Druids existed on Mann, as an Ogham inscription on a stone found at Ballaqueeny near Port St Mary railway station refers to *dovaidona maqi droata* or 'Dovaidu son of the Druid'. Islands were considered to be places of special significance for Druidism and Anglesey was a Druid stronghold until a particularly bloody Roman invasion and massacre in AD60. It seems likely that the surviving Druids fled across the Irish Sea to the Isle of Man and Ireland.

In many communities Druids were considered to be more important than the nominal leaders. They and their religion were surrounded in mystique, partly because they themselves created mystery by instructing their acolytes in secret and writing nothing down, and partly because

A Brief History of the Isle of Man

they left very few artefacts so we know little about them; the Manx for Druid, *druaightagh*, is the same as the Manx for magician. The Druid religion was based on the natural world so they built no temples and nothing structural therefore remains to be found. Instead Druids held their religious ceremonies in sacred groves of trees – oak for preference – or by hallowed springs or pools. Spooyt Vane, near Kirk Michael, is traditionally one such site.

Human sacrifice appears to have been practised in the Druidical religion although their very firm belief in an afterlife seems to have led some sacrificial victims to volunteer

Gallarus Oratory, County Kerry, Ireland. Built between the sixth and ninth centuries using techniques first developed by Neolithic tomb makers, the Oratory has one door and a tiny window. The Manx keeills may have been similar

for the role; ancient texts written by Roman historians, for example, seem to suggest as much. As well as sacrificing people and animals Druids also placed votive offerings of finely wrought swords, daggers, etc., into sacred pools. The two chief festival days when large tribal assemblies took place were Beltain and Samhain. The former took place at the beginning of May to herald the start of summer, the latter at the beginning of November to usher in winter. Druids were skilled herbalists and used their knowledge to produce what would now be called hallucinogenic drugs to aid the celebration of the festivals; the myths of witches and wizards being able to fly probably stems from the use of such drugs.

Into the Druidical society came Christian missionaries from Ireland and two of St Patrick's disciples, Romulus and Conindrus, are generally

Lag ny Keeilley. South of Niarbyl and a mile walk from Eairy Cushlin along an old pack horse track it is the site of the most remote keeill on Mann. Despite its remoteness its burial ground was occasionally still used into the nineteenth century

Interior of St Adamnan's, better known as Lonan Old Church. The building shows many similarities with the Irish Oratory. For hundreds of years St Adamnan's has been lit by oil lamps as it has no electricity

credited with establishing Christianity on the Isle of Man in AD447. The Celtic Christian church was not at first under the rule of the Church of Rome and was organised rather differently. Monasteries could contain both men and women and the two sexes could marry and raise children. Those seeking for a meditative spiritual life could become anchorites, living alone but still serving God within the local community. Such solitary holy men – and they were almost always men – were known as Culdees. Each built a cabbal or early chapel, with a priest's cell attached. Cabbals are small, rectangular buildings sometimes no more than about five feet tall, built of sods, roofed with turf and with a floor dug away to a depth of between one and two feet. The tiny buildings were situated at the eastern end of a small enclosure the whole of which was set on top of a low mound. As the cabbals were so small, services would almost certainly have been held out of doors.

Cabbals were probably introduced in the middle of the fifth century, while keeills took over or were developed in the sixth. Keeills differ little in design from cabbals but are often slightly larger, have a single window in addition to a door – cabbals lack a window – and are generally built of stone. There are thought to be the remains of over 200 keeills on Mann and many parish churches have been expanded from old keeills which stood on the same site. Lonan Old Church dedicated to St Adamnan's, for example, was originally called Keeill-ny-Traie or the church by the shore. Because the Culdees were solitary and austere, cabbals and keeills were often in lonely or remote locations.

Attached to each keeill was a burial ground or *ruillick*, much the same as more recent churches have their churchyard. Stone-lined graves called lintel graves have been discovered, such as the one uncovered by the archaeologists from Channel 4's Time Team when they dug the Speke Farm keeill on the seventh fairway of the Mount Murray golf course about a mile north west of Port Soderick. One of the lintel graves included the extremely well-preserved remains of a woman, and included a knot of plaited hair. Carbon dating revealed that the burial took place around 590 AD, making it probably the oldest Christian burial found on the island. Lintel graves took a long time to fashion and so it's likely that only the most important people – priests, leaders of the community, heads of households, etc. – would have been buried in them. During the Celtic period women were considered to hold virtually equal status with men and could be powerful individuals in their own right. The fact that the Mount Murray grave contained a woman does not lessen her status or that of the likely importance of lintel

A Brief History of the Isle of Man

graves. As well as being lined with stone, the grave was covered by a stone slab possibly with another stone erected at its head. Such a slab may well have been incised with a cross and simple inscription.

Maughold is unusually rich in keeills which are also placed unusually close together. Not only has the church been developed from a keeill, the remains of three others still exist in the churchyard, with the position of a fourth marked by a short granite pillar. Maughold churchyard is particularly large and occupies the site of an important Celtic monastery which enclosed and subsumed the earlier keeills. The arrangement of the buildings seems to demonstrate the transition from a Christianity based on isolated priests serving the spiritual needs of local families, to a Christianity based on specialist communities gathered at spiritual centres. The Maughold arrangement is particularly rare however, as the monastery has been dated to the sixth century which is about the time when keeills were flourishing on the island. Were the keeill system and monastic system rivals, perhaps representing two different interpretations of the Christian message? Or did the monastery and possibly others like it, act as something like base stations for the various outlying keeills?

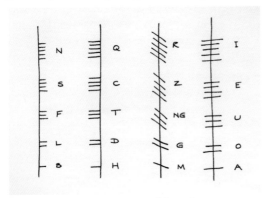

Ogham script. Ogham is read from bottom to top or left to right. The first twenty letters of the alphabet are generally agreed, although extra letters appear to have been added at a later date or might have had regional significance

The Manx crosses and Celtic art

The early Christians left unique evidence of their faith in the impressive number of carved stone slabs, generally referred to as the Manx crosses. The earliest crosses date from around the fifth century, when Christianity first arrived in Mann. Fittingly, as the faith first came from Ireland, some inscriptions on the Manx crosses are written in Ogham, a system of writing which was widely used in Ireland between the fourth and the eighth centuries. Most unusually, the latest inscription, also found at Mount Murray, appears to be written in an Ogham version of Scots Gaelic from around the thirteenth century.

The Ogham alphabet is based on a series of straight lines marked across a single unifying line, making it ideal for marking on anything with a straight edge. It is thought to have possibly been developed from a tallying system which used notched sticks to indicate quantities. Although virtually all Ogham script survives as stone inscriptions, it was more commonly used on wooden rods, fence posts and trees. Ogham is read as the tree grows, i.e. from bottom to top, although when inscribed on a stone it can reach the top and go down the other side. Several of the Manx crosses have Ogham inscriptions and there are some good examples in the Manx Museum.

Dunloe Ogham stone from Coolmagort, Ireland

Despite tales of warlike Celtic tribesmen, there was no race as far as we know who called themselves the Celts. The name has been given to a loosely-related group of tribes which probably shared a similar language, customs and religion. The Iron Age is noted for the richness of its decorative items and ornament was important in the clothing and utensils of the time. It is during the Iron Age that decoration began to develop into the sophisticated patterns of what is now generally known as Celtic art or design.

At first the decoration was of swirling lines which flowed but did not overlap or interlace. The intricate knotwork which appears magnificently on many of the Manx crosses was

Cross-slab from Glen Roy now at Lonan Old Church. It shows the early flowing patterns which pre-date knot work and which are more purely Celtic. The shape in the centre is thought to represent a spoon or baptism ladle

introduced in the sixth century almost certainly by Christian missionaries and probably from Ireland – the knotwork was at first used to illustrate religious texts. The new possibilities for overlapping and intertwining decoration were quickly incorporated into the older Celtic style of swirling patterns where the lines did not cross. A further layer was added to the decoration by the Viking influence. Many of the Scandinavian designs of the time were illustrative of Viking sagas, etc., and were populated with stylised representations of mythical beasts. Celtic designers were again influenced by the new ideas without relinquishing their old templates. Consequently any knotwork which incorporates animal shapes shows the influence of three different traditions; early Celtic in the swirling patterns, Christian in the knotwork, Norse in the animals.

In England and Wales, the Iron Age is said to have ended abruptly at 43 BC when the Romans invaded. Of course the lives of most of the ordinary people continued much as they had been before, but natives of England and Wales couldn't escape the influence of the Roman conquerors. The Isle of Man, Scotland and Ireland were not subject to Roman invasion and so the Iron Age way of life lingered there until the next wave of invaders came, this time from the north. The Vikings.

CHAPTER 3

INVADERS FROM THE NORTH

Unlike the gradual development which the Isle of Man experienced over the preceding millennia, the ninth century saw an abrupt change when the Vikings invaded. The first Viking raids on the British Isles were made on the north-east coast of England at the monastery of Lindisfarne in 793. A tentative sortie had been made on Northumberland about four years earlier, but, according to the *Anglo Saxon Chronicle*, on 8 January 793 'the harrying of the heathen miserably destroyed God's church in Lindisfarne by rapine and slaughter.' Five years later in 798 the first raiders arrived in the Irish Sea, and attacked and burned the buildings on St Patrick's Isle. The Scandinavian invaders were superb seafarers and easily recognised the strategic importance of the Isle of Man, not only as a base from which to conduct raids, but also as a trading centre for the neighbouring islands. Their conquest of Mann was rapid and virtually complete by 800.

So who were the Vikings? Why did they come to the islands around Britain at all? And why now?

Warriors from the sea

Firstly, although some of the invaders called themselves Vikings, they weren't using the word to describe their clan or tribe, but rather their activity. In Old Norse a *vik* is a creek, bay or river estuary and therefore a good place to attack. The word *viking* can be used as a noun meaning a raid from the sea or as a verb, hence 'going viking', while a *vikingr* is a sea warrior. Vikings were therefore seafaring raiders, but very few of them were what could be called professionals, i.e. full-time warriors.

Above and left: Viking warriors inside and outside the House of Manannan, Peel

Most were farmers looking to eke out their living. They might, for example, become a vikingr for a season or two before settling down, or return to raiding after a bad harvest. Only a few of the Norsemen were Vikings at any one time but most were or had been Vikings some of the time.

The fact that Vikings were part-time raiders by no means meant that they were not effective. The Norse culture extolled the virtues of warfare and proficiency in arms while prizing courage and indifference to danger. And forget the picturesque idea of horned helmets. Helmets with horns might look impressive but would be difficult to make – how would you secure horn to iron? – and impractical to wear as the horns would make the helmet heavy, unwieldy and prone to

Viking ship Hugin, Broadstairs, England. Sailed from Denmark in 1949 by 53 Danes, the design of the Hugin is probably very similar to those which were used to invade Mann

catch on things. Vikings were ruthlessly practical and if Wagner did not invent such headgear then the tourist industry probably did. Horned helmets would catch sword blades not deflect them as did the iron skull-cap helmets which the Vikings actually favoured.

At the beginning Vikings raided Britain for plunder, pure and simple. Raiding was not only a way of increasing an individual or group's portable wealth, but also, according to the Norse society's priorities at the time, did so in a praiseworthily heroic manner. Done once and successfully, rivalry and copy-cat activities would make sure that the number and severity of raids increased.

Various suggestions ranging from population expansion to economic prosperity have been made as to why the raids started when they did. The truth is that we don't know what prompted the Norsemen to start invading their neighbours. With such a long coastline they must have become excellent sailors very early in their history. Most men carried a spear and a dagger, the former of which was mainly used as a long-range stabbing implement although they could also be thrown. Swords were rarer as they were costly to make and so were a sign of high status, while battleaxes were only developed towards the end of the Viking Age. Weapons were not only carried to be used in anger but as a way of demonstrating their owners' wealth and status and so were often highly decorated. All free men were expected to own weapons, and tribal leaders were expected to provide them for their men.

From rich pickings to a good place to live
The gulf stream makes Britain much warmer than its continental neighbours and Scandinavia in particular is cold. Britain's ambient temperature and relatively high rainfall makes farming land richer and more fertile than most of the land east of it. Whether trading

A Brief History of the Isle of Man

or raiding the Norsemen must have returned home extolling the virtues of the warmer climate and the productivity of the land. Most Vikings were farmers and such good farming land was probably a temptation. Having faced them in arms, the Norsemen also knew that the land's inhabitants were no match for their own military prowess. After only a couple of years of pillaging the raiders became the invaders.

Land in the Isle of Man was, and largely still is, organised into treens. Each treen is an area defined within natural borders such as streams and cliffs, plus boundaries developed by custom such as paths and stonewalls. Treens vary in size from less than 200 to more than 600 acres, with most around 400 acres. The derivation of the word causes much debate, but it seems likely that 'treen' is connected with the Scottish Gaelic *tir-unga*, with *tir* being land and *unga* or *uinge* meaning an ingot of a particular weight. A *tir-unga* was a unit of land decided by the revenue it generated rather than by its size. Similarly a treen is also a fiscal unit, and therefore also varies in size; more could be produced from good land and so the same amount of revenue from agriculture could be expected from a small treen encompassing good land as that from a large treen containing poor land.

Each treen was divided into four farms, known as quarterlands. Again the extent of the quarterland farm was determined by the revenue of the land and not its size, so, although most are around 90 acres, quarterlands may not be an exact division of the treen. There is also much evidence, although it's not conclusive, to suggest that each treen contained its own keeill. If such be the case, it points to the treens being a Celtic organisation of land units and therefore predating the Viking invaders. Whether that is true or not, the Norsemen certainly used the arrangement. Most treens have Norse names while most quarterlands are known by Gaelic names; the nomenclature emphasises the dominance of the Norsemen and provides an interesting insight into the relationship between the invaders and the newly-conquered people.

Tynwald Hill, St John's. Every year on 5 July the Manx parliament meets to proclaim the new laws (see Appendix 3)

Most of the Vikings who settled in the Isle of Man came originally from Norway. It is noticeable that the invading forces from Scandinavia seemed to divide into three groups. Invaders from what is now Norway settled in Mann, Ireland and south Wales, Swedes settled along the west coast of Scotland and Danes in north and west England. It appears that there was either some sort of prior agreement between the groups as to who had what, or they preferred to fight softer targets rather than each other.

Most of the political and legal structure of the Isle of Man can be traced directly to the organisation of the Norsemen. Communities in Scandinavia lived in small tribal groups isolated by forest and fjord. To ensure that tribal harmony was maintained and larger issues discussed, the free men of the community met periodically to debate, affirm, amend or add to existing tribal laws. In Norse the meeting was known as a *thing*. Several communities coming

St John's Church, St John's. Integral to the Tynwald Hill ceremony, dignitaries process along the path from the church to the hill

together for a joint meeting on larger issues constituted an *all-thing*. The meeting had little to do with governance but concentrated on legislation, i.e. was concerned with law rather than politics. The ancient tradition is echoed today in the names of the parliaments of Iceland (*Althingi*), Norway (*Storting*), Finland (*Lagting*), Denmark (*Folketing*), and the Faroe Isles (*Løgting*). Even Shetland and Orkney had their parliaments, both at places called Tingwall. Only in the Isle of Man is the tradition unbroken in the oldest continuous parliament in the world – Tynwald. And, even today, the legal rather than political nature of the assembly is emphasised in its formal designation: The Court of Tynwald.

The assembly field where a thing took place was called the *thing-völlr*, which is where Tynwald gets its name. The leaders of the assembly met on a low hill which was linked by a processional way stretching eastwards to a courthouse which doubled as a place of worship. The whole was surrounded by banks. Traditionally the mound included a handful of earth brought from each tribal territory, so that all tribal representatives could think of themselves as being on their homeground and, perhaps more importantly, be governed by the laws of hospitality. Tynwald Hill in St John's is said to contain earth drawn from every parish in the island and is still linked by a processional way to St John's Church, consecrated in 1849 but replacing a much older series of religious buildings.

The Royal Chapel in St John's is unique for two reasons; not only is it the only Christian church where a government meets (albeit only once a year on Tynwald Day), but it is also the only Christian church with an area which is unconsecrated. The area where members of the House of Keys sit is not consecrated so that any non-Christian members can be accommodated (see Appendix 3).

Midsummer was a time when isolated communities got together to celebrate and it would have

Tynwald Hill, near West Baldwin Reservoir. The Manx parliament met here in 1428

saved much travelling if a *thing* was held at the same time. Tynwald still meets on 5 July, Old Midsummer's Day. No record exists stating when Tynwald first began, although as an established part of Norse culture, it's likely that local *things*, rather like a meeting of the local council, would have been introduced

The Braaid. Remains of one of the two rectangular Norse buildings on the site. The third building is a Celtic roundhouse, probably taken over by the Norse

almost as soon as the Norsemen established settlements in 800. The island celebrated 1,000 years of Tynwald in 1979, which suggests that the national *thing* was established, or at least formalised by 979 when the island owed allegiance to Earl Haakan Sigurdsson, King of Norway (see Appendix I). Sites of other Tynwalds, national as well as local, must have existed, and two are thought to have been identified. One is near West Baldwin Reservoir north of St Luke's church, appropriately enough on the Millennium Way, while the other is at Cronk Urley upstream from Glen Wyllin on a small hill to the east of the current A3.

The Viking way of life

Unlike Celtic round houses, Norse houses were rectangular with pitched roofs made of timber framing filled with wattle and daub. The hearth was a circle of stones placed in the centre, while each thatched roof had a gap in the eaves to allow the prevailing wind to blow the smoke away. Fire was started by striking a flint to cause sparks to fall onto a piece of charred flax. The flax glowed and was helped into full flame by gentle blowing. All the materials would have been stored in a pouch hung from a leather belt.

Leather and hide was a very important resource for the Vikings. Clothing, particularly that worn by men, would have been made of leather, shutters and doors were hung on leather hinges, and hide was used in shield making. Iron helmets, although much prized, were difficult and costly to make and close-fitting leather caps were probably worn by many of the rank and file. Thick hide is even said to have been used as armour and was reputedly very effective. Leather is a remarkably good barrier against projectiles; even Second World War bomb disposal teams sometimes wore leather jerkins as body armour.

The popular image of Vikings is of wild-haired, quarrelsome savages. Quarrelsome they were but were also fastidious when it came to personal grooming. Accounts from the time say, often critically, that Vikings regularly washed and combed their hair, washed their faces and hands daily, and usually bathed about once a week. Hair for both men and women was worn shoulder length or longer – short hair was a sign of thraldom or slavery – and unwashed hair was only tolerated as a sign of mourning. Excavations of grave goods in Scandinavia suggest that both sexes carried personal combs, and men also usually had a rigid comb case made from bone or antler to protect their comb from damage. Women are thought to have carried their combs inside a cloth pouch.

Ornamentation was as important to people then as it is now. Cloaks were held in place by finely wrought pins, hair was braided and both sexes wore jewellery. Bead necklaces were particularly prized and one of the richest tenth-century female graves outside Scandinavia was found in 1984 during an archaeological excavation on St Patrick's Isle. Now known as The Pagan Lady, the grave's occupant had with her an extraordinary variety of high-quality beads, probably originally strung as a necklace. A total of seventy three were found, in a variety of shapes, the largest almost an inch and a half in diameter. Most are of different coloured glass, but a few are of amber and jet. The amber would have come from the shores of either the Baltic or the North Sea, but the only source of jet open to the people of the time was Whitby, North Yorkshire, on the east coast of England.

Commemorative stamp from 1986 showing the Pagan Lady's necklace

The Norsemen's seafaring skill is well known and boats of similar style were used for both raiding and trading. The Viking ship as most think of it probably came into that form by the late eighth century. It had the advantage of size, which allowed for ocean travel, but combined considerable size with a shallow draught, sometimes as little as eighteen inches, which enabled ships to be navigated far up rivers and beached on a variety of coastlines. Sails which swivelled to catch the prevailing wind complemented oars which gave extra speed and manoeuvrability. The ships were steered not by a rudder, but by a single oar mounted on the starboard near the stern. This incidentally is where the word starboard comes from; it's the steering board or steerboard. The steering oar was mounted on the right so, to avoid fouling it, the ship was moored with its left side to the land or port, hence port and starboard. Ships were built in various sizes, but a typical raiding vessel had a crew of about fifty seated on benches on open decks. Fierce figureheads looked out from bow and stern and the circular shields carried by the warriors could be mounted along the sides for defence; they would be removed while at sea. The whole was a light, fast, flexible ship equally capable of carrying cargo across the Atlantic to Greenland, or raiders up the Neb River to St John's.

The size and shape of at least one sort of Viking ship was clearly indicated when the ship burial was excavated at Balladoole just west of Castletown. The original timbers had rotted away, but the large number of clenched boat nails clearly indicated where it had lain. From them the vessel's original length was calculated at about thirty-six feet. It could have carried an estimated cargo of around four tons and probably needed a minimum crew of five. The boat may have been used to transport lightweight cargo and may have traded between the Isle of Man and the surrounding islands.

Some of the Viking invaders may have brought their wives with them but many married native Celtic women, possibly the daughters of the families they conquered. Children would then have been brought up in a mix of two cultures and perhaps also a mix of two religions, Christianity and paganism. Many of the defeated people would probably have been enslaved

A Brief History of the Isle of Man

to work the land they formerly owned. Vikings distinguished between unfree servants of their own tribes which they called *þræll* or thralls, and slaves or *anauð* which were captured in raids. Both thralls and slaves did the hard and dirty jobs which no-one else wanted, but slaves were also considered valuable trading items, constituting much of their master's portable property.

As property, slaves were also considered valid grave goods to be buried with their master when he died. At Balladoole, the ship carried a finely-dressed man, together with numerous high-quality grave goods including a circular shield, knife, fire-making equipment, spurs and a horse's bridle and bit. At the dead man's feet lay the remains of an adult woman, without grave goods. Even more conclusive proof that slaves kept their masters company in death, is the woman included with the burial of a high-status Viking at Ballateare, just south of Jurby. Excavation revealed not only his remains but also that of a woman who had been killed by a blow from a sharp weapon across the back of her skull. As well as animal sacrifices other chattels included in the grave were three spears, indicated by the surviving iron spearheads, a knife, sword, scabbard and shield. The shield boss was excavated and the wooden remains of the shield itself showed that it had once been painted in red white and black.

Unusually, at Balladoole, no weaponry appears to have been included in the grave, unless it had been removed by grave robbers. At Ballateare the iron sword was decorated with silver inlay and had been deliberately broken into three pieces, possibly as a symbol that the living hand of its former master could no longer wield it or perhaps, more mundanely, to discourage grave robbers. The breaks might even have been to deprive the dead man of the use of his sword if he returned as one of the *draugr* or walking dead. According to Viking belief, *draugr* were corpses who lived in the burial mound, often beneath a rock, and who wanted to return and interfere with the living they had left behind.

Multicultural

The Vikings, unlike the Celtic Irish, placed little reliance on written records, preferring instead to rely on a bardic oral tradition to pass on stories and history. They were not however illiterate. They used runes. In Old Norse the word 'rune' means letter or text. Runes gained their aura of slight

Viking ship burial, Balladoole looking inland towards South Barrule. The stones are not original but placed to mark where the ship rested (see also front cover)

mysticism as the word also means secret in some of the Old Germanic languages.

Just as the word 'alphabet' comes from the first two Greek letters alpha and beta so the runic equivalent is known as the futhark from the first six runes in it. Runes are difficult to read because there are a number of different variations depending on age and country. Just before the Viking Age the number of characters in the futhark had been reduced from twenty four to sixteen; towards the end of the

Runic futhark. The futhark of different countries and times differs; this is the Norwegian version of what is known as the Younger Futhark and was used from about 800-1200

Viking Age, around 1100, it was expanded again. From around 800 Denmark, Sweden and Norway each had a slightly different variation of runes, while the futhark of what was to become Germany differed again. Although many runic descriptions remain on Mann, there are not enough variations to indicate particular areas from which the Viking invaders principally came.

Reading runes is made even more difficult as they might legitimately be carved back-to-front or upside down; the early inscriptions were even occasionally made to be read from right to left. Like ogham (see chapter 2) most runes were made up of straight lines which made letters easier to carve into stone, wood, bone or metal. Runes can be and were used for everything from gravestones to graffiti, and runic inscriptions have been found on items as disparate as coins, jewellery, memorial tablets, swords, and fortune-tellers' wands.

As the years went by and the Norsemen became part of the island's indigenous people, so aspects of their culture merged with the older Celtic culture onto which they had been grafted. The amalgamation of the two is obvious even today in the names given to various places around Mann. A few, such as Rushen, pre-date the Norse influence. Many are pure Norse, such as Foxdale which has nothing to do with the animal but is a corruption of *fossdal* or waterfall valley; the German *Tal* or valley has the same root. Some names appear in both languages, for example Ballaglass (Gaelic) and Grenaby (Norse). *Balla*, sometimes *Balley*, is the equivalent of the Norse *byr* and means farm or homestead. *Glass* is the green of plants, while *grön*, similar to the *grün* of German, simply means green. Ballaglass and Grenaby both therefore mean Green Farm.

Perhaps most revealing are those names which combine

Broken cross slab, Bride. The runes are clearly visible on the right side and mean 'Druian, son of Dugald, raised this cross to the memory of Athmaoil his wife'

elements of both Gaelic and Norse. 'By', for example, was a Norse prefix given only to important places to indicate their superiority. It appears, slightly transmuted, at the beginning of Bemahague in Onchan. The name combines Gaelic and Norse elements which probably means that it was a place important to the indigenous people, and then taken over by Viking invaders. A rough original would be 'By-Mac-Thaidhg', or 'important farm of the son of Taig'. It's been considered an important

Runes used as a modern decoration on Skandia House, Douglas. They are in fact a simple address and translate as 'Skandia Hufudhstradkr Maun', or 'Skandia, Howstrake, Mann'

place for over a millennium and is still considered such today. Now it's more commonly known as Government House. It is the official residence of the Lieutenant Governor of the island.

The inscriptions and designs which survive in the Manx crosses on the island also emphasise the mix of the two cultures. Several crosses from the tenth and eleventh centuries, for instance, combine pagan and Christian scenes. A particularly fine example can be found at St Andrew's church, Kirk Andreas. Known as the Thorwald cross, it is named not after any of the figures carved on the cross, but after the man who erected it. His name appears in the runes which – unusually – run down rather than up the side.

The appearance of pagan symbolism around a Christian cross would be considered incongruous today, but the people of the time were obviously quite happy with the juxtaposition. Not a great deal is known about Viking religious practices, although the great sagas tell us a lot about Norse mythology and the pagan gods. The Vikings arrived on the island as pagans, with pagan beliefs and burial customs, but soon adopted the faith of their new land. There must have been considerable pressure to accept Christianity as, apart from the faith of the conquered people, rulers and traders across the water in England and Ireland were also predominantly Christian and a shared faith made transactions less problematic.

The Thorwald cross, Andreas. The figure under the arm of the cross is Odin. On his right shoulder is a raven and his right foot is in the mouth of the Fenris wolf which is about to swallow him

Viking acceptance of Christianity might also have been easier for them as the Norsemen had many gods; the Christian God was just one more. Pagan burial customs of ship burials and barrows were replaced by Christian burial customs of graves and grave markers, yet the latter still displayed many of the pagan myths of their Nordic commissioners. Particularly interesting is the burial ground on St Patrick's Isle. It started being used in the seventh century as a Christian burial ground, was used for pagan burials around the tenth century during the Viking incursion, before reverting again to containing Christian graves.

The oldest surviving building on St Patrick's Isle and one of the oldest on Mann is the tenth century round tower built in the Irish style. Towers similar in appearance exist on Douglas Head and Langness but are much more recent and were built at the beginning of the nineteenth century as a guide to shipping and to mark harbour entrances. There are over seventy mediaeval round towers left in Britain, and the sites of a further thirty are known, although the towers themselves don't survive. Almost all such round towers were in Ireland. The three exceptions are the one on St Patrick's Isle on Mann and one each at Brechin and Abernethy in Scotland.

Above: Irish-style round tower, Peel Castle
Right: Irish round tower, Dunkineely, Donegal, Ireland

Why the towers were built at all is still something of a mystery. Invariably they were part of a religious foundation, usually near the western end of the monastery's most important church, with entrances to church and tower facing each other. Most were about a hundred feet high and fifty in circumference, with a conical roof at first of wood and slate, but later of stone. In Irish Gaelic such towers are called *clog teach* or bell house (*clag* or *clagg* is Manx for bell), which suggests that part at least of their function was to house bells to call the faithful and sound the alarm. The technology of bell casting had been discovered in the eighth century and was often jealously guarded by monastic communities.

Various esoteric suggestions have been made about other uses for such towers including houses for hermits, gnomons in the middle of huge sundials and early signal stations. The suggestion that the St Patrick's Isle round tower was built as a look out against Viking invaders is unlikely to be true, or at least is unlikely to be quite that simple. Apart from representing a huge amount of work – if the Manx wanted a look-out station, why not use one of the nearby hills? – Vikings had settled in Mann almost a century before the tower was built. The Manx and Irish Vikings were originally from Norway however and, certainly in Ireland, occasionally

A Brief History of the Isle of Man

fought off waves of incoming Vikings from Denmark who were settling in England. The Isle of Man could well have been caught in the middle. The tower obviously had some sort of defensive role, as the doorway is about ten feet above ground level, accessible originally by a ladder which was hauled up after the last defender had scrambled in. The arrangement was effective against casual tribal raiders but could not withstand a deliberate and concerted attack from a force intending to take over the area.

The political landscape

It is something of an understatement to say that the Viking period is not one which is noted for its peace. Fathers fought against sons, brothers against each other and, under the still largely tribal organisation of the society at the time, ordinary men were dragged away from their farms and into the fighting. Not that they'd probably have objected too much. As we've seen, fighting skills were highly valued among the Norsemen and a good Viking would have grown bored with too much peace. Although usually on the western edge of the combat zone, the Isle of Man was often called on to supply men, arms and ships for the various conflicts in the Scandinavian holdings. Fighting also occurred sporadically in Dublin, which was one of the most important Viking settlements in the world. Although strategically important the island itself knew an uneasy peace for almost three hundred years after the Norsemen first arrived. That all changed with the arrival of Godred Crovan.

Brought up on Mann, Godred Crovan was the local boy made good. He had left the island, but in 1079 returned in arms. He must have been fairly determined as he was twice defeated. Third time lucky he planned a trap. During the night he sailed up the river at Ramsey – the name *Rhumsaa* means wild garlic river – landed with three hundred men and hid them in the trees on the slopes of Sky Hill. *The Chronicles of the Kings of Man and the Isles*, written by the monks of Rushen Abbey in the twelfth and thirteenth centuries, explains what happened next:

'At dawn the Manxmen formed up in battle order and after a massive charge joined battle with Godred. When the battle was raging vehemently, the three hundred men rose from their place of hiding at the rear of the Manxmen and began to weaken their resistance, and they compelled them to flee. Now when they saw themselves defeated without any place for them to escape to, for the tide had filled the riverbed at Ramsey and the enemy were pressing constantly from the other side, those who were left begged Godred with pitiful cries to spare them their lives.'

The Manx form of the name Godred is Goree, and Godred Crovan is the King Gorree, or King Orry of Manx myth (see chapter 9). It is Godred who is credited with establishing much of island's legislature and governance. He confirmed the *thing* assembly – Tynwald – and is said to have

Site of the Battle of Sky Hill. Godred Crovan defeated the Manx here in 1079

divided the island into its six sheadings, although there is little evidence that it was Godred who did so. The word sheading is most often thought to come from the Norse *skeid*, an ocean-going warship with thirty benches, which needed sixty rowers and therefore had a crew of about eighty. At this period the *skeid* was used extensively, and tended to be the ship of choice for wealthy earls; the eleventh century equivalent of a sports team touring coach if you like. It's likely therefore that *skeid* would be popular among Godred Crovan and his followers. Sheadings are thought to have the responsibility of providing a specified number of men to man a warship. More prosaically the word *scheding*, with or without the 'h', meant 'division' in the English of Godred's time – the modern verb 'to shed' comes from the same root. Whatever the derivation, the sheadings have formed the basis of the island's organisation and administration ever since.

As a reward to the loyal followers who won him victory, Godred granted plunder to those who wanted to leave and land in the south of the island to those who preferred to settle. Then as now the best agricultural land was considered as being in the south, that is the south of the island as divided along the mountain range from North to South Barrule, rather than along the Douglas to Peel valley.

Godred's dispossession of the native Manx from their land rebounded on the incomers nineteen years later. Civil war was fought between northerners – the natives – and southerners – the come-overs – at Santwat, thought to be not far from Patrick near Peel. The *Chronicles* state categorically that the victory went to the north, but other sources put the south as victorious, which Manx tradition appears to endorse. Virtually everyone agrees, however, that the victors at Santwat won because they were helped by their women. Watching the battle from the hills and seeing it go badly with their menfolk, wives and daughters swept down to fight, and the extra numbers carried the day. However, it's Celtic women, the pre-Viking natives, who traditionally fight next to their men when needed, so perhaps the Chronicles were right after all.

The battle at Santwat in 1098 had a lasting effect on Mann almost by accident. King Magnus III of Norway, recent conqueror of Orkney and future conqueror of Anglesey, landed on St Patrick's Isle shortly after the battle, when the bodies of the dead were still unburied. Divided and exhausted, no-one was in any state to defend themselves and Magnus easily proclaimed himself king. The fortunate timing sounds like the work of spies or even an *agent provocateur*, but nothing remains in the records of the time to indicate such.

Known as Magnus *Barfot*, the king's soubriquet means barefoot or barelegs and is thought to have come from his habit of wearing a tunic to the knees without the trews which would normally go underneath it. King Magnus built a hall on St Patrick's Isle insisting that the people from Galloway, the part of Scotland nearest to Mann, should supply the timber to build it. By similar means he stated that the Isle of Man should pay tribute money to Norway and acknowledge the Norwegian king as an overlord in perpetuity. It's always difficult to refuse a 'request' from someone who's shown he's quite capable of taking what he wants and a lot more besides. Magnus couldn't take Ireland though. Despite a treaty with Muirchertach II, King of Ireland, Magnus invaded. And was killed.

'On his [Magnus's] death the chieftains of the Isles sent for Olaf, son of Godred Crovan, of whom we have previously made mention, who was at that time living at the court of Henry, King of England…' The Manx *Chronicles* describe the succession of Olaf as peaceful and popular, and his long reign proved to be both.

The growth of Christianity

It was during the reign of Olaf I that Rushen Abbey was founded. In 1124, Stephen de

Blois, Count of Mortain, Lord of Lancaster and later King of England founded St Mary's Abbey in north-west England. St Mary's original home was at Tulketh near Preston in Lancashire, England, but three years later the house was moved to a site on the Furness peninsula. In 1134, the *Chronicles* say: 'King Olaf granted to Ivo, abbot of Furness, part of his land in Mann to establish an abbey in a place which is called Rushen.' Rushen Abbey was the third of seven daughter houses established for Furness, the others being Calder and Swineshead in England,

and Fermoy, Holy Cross, Corcumruadh and Inislaunaght in Ireland. At the time of its founding Furness was part of the Savigniac congregation, but when two orders merged in 1147, Furness and its daughter houses became absorbed into the Cistercian Order.

On a good day the coast of Mann is visible from Furness. Stephen and Olaf had both lived at the court of King Henry I of England and could easily have known each other, possibly well. It's not impossible that the granting of Manx land to this particular house at this particular time was partly the result of friendship or alliance between two powerful men.

It seems odd that one of the

Furness Abbey, Cumbria, now under the care of English Heritage. Photograph © English Heritage

island's most important religious foundations was established on Mann at a time when the Viking influence was so strong, but many of those of Viking descent, including the king himself, had by now adopted the new faith. Other monastic foundations were also established on Mann, including Douglas Priory, now known as The Nunnery, and a Franciscan Friary at Bemaken near Ballabeg and not far from the railway line to Port Erin. In addition, grants of land were made to religious foundations in England and Ireland, including land around Maughold made by Godred II to St Bees Priory in Cumbria, England. No religious foundation was as influential as Rushen Abbey however, and King Olaf himself was, according to the *Chronicles* 'devout and enthusiastic in matters of religion and was welcome both to God and men.'

The establishment of Rushen Abbey must have been fraught with difficulty, even if the locals were co-operative – and there was no reason why they should be. The first abbot and twelve monks would have come from Furness and local farmers would have been deprived of all or part of their land to make room for the new abbey.

The church tower and rebuilt example of part of the cloister walk, Rushen Abbey

The monastic buildings were probably built originally of wood, but replaced in stone as soon as possible. Materials taken to build the abbey, fuel for its fires, and fish and produce for its food would deplete local sources. More importantly, however, the monks would have expected to recruit locally for novices and lay brothers, and newcomers and locals would probably have had no language in common. The monks would have Latin, possibly Norman French, and probably the local Middle English dialect spoken around Furness. The Manx would speak Celtic and Norse. Perhaps traders or one of the island's priests acted as interpreter?

The rule laid down by St Benedict stated that foundations such as Rushen Abbey must be self supporting, offer hospitality to all who needed it, care for the sick and the poor and be places for prayer and study. Abbey lands would usually be worked by lay brothers or tenant farmers, to allow the monks more time for their devotions. Such lands became extensive as more and more were donated by various patrons over the years. Rushen Abbey eventually came to own land in the area east of Sulby as well as around Peel, Port St Mary and Port Erin

The monastic foundation formed one branch of Christianity, the bishoprics and parishes another. The first diocesan bishop recorded as exercising jurisdiction over Mann was Roolwer, when the island acknowledged the King of England as overlord; Roolwer appears to have been a suffragan bishop of York and was in post at around 1050. A century later Mann's allegiance was demanded by the King of Norway so it was reasonable to expect the bishop to be a Norwegian appointment. All the lands ruled by Norway were therefore incorporated into one huge see (see Appendix 2).

At various times during the Viking occupation of Mann, the Hebrides, Shetland, Orkney, Iceland, Greenland and the Faroe Islands also came under Scandinavian rule. The Norsemen knew the Hebrides as the Southern Islands, which in Norse is *Suðoer* (Orkney and Shetland

Bishopscourt, near Kirk Michael. It was the official residence of the Bishops of Sodor and Man from the twelfth century until 1979. It is now a private house

A Brief History of the Isle of Man

Roolwer, the first Bishop of Mann. The stained glass window is in Maughold Church

GO THE GLORY OF GOD AND IN MEMORY
OF ROOLWER FIRST RECORDED BISHOP
TO WHOM WHO WAS BURIED HERE CIRCA 1061

were the Northern Islands or *Norðoer*). The head of the newly-created see was given the title Bishop of Sodor and Man, so it is probably from *Suðoer* that the diocese of Sodor and Man gets the first part of its name.

The creation of the see was something of a shotgun marriage as two archbishops, one of York in England, one of Nidaros (Trondheim) in Norway, both claimed the right to consecrate new bishops. To add to the confusion, the charter by which Olaf I granted land for the foundation of Rushen Abbey, also grants to the abbey the right to choose the bishop of Sodor and Man. Despite the fact that the king had no authority to grant such a right, Rushen's mother house Furness Abbey, and even the leaders of the Cistercian Order in France seized the opportunity eagerly, and occasionally tried to appoint bishops, with greater or lesser success, over the next hundred years or so. All the jockeying for position sometimes meant that Mann had two or more bishops, each appointed by a different power claiming the right to do so.

Until 1974, Bishopscourt was the official residence of the Bishop of Sodor and Man. It is possibly the only building on the island known to have been continuously occupied since the thirteenth century and believed to have been so for at least a century before than that. Structurally the central tower, now known as the Orry or Peele Tower, remains very much as it was built. Tradition states that it was originally built as a defensive residence for the king; the king in question is not specified but could be Olaf I, founder of Rushen Abbey and known to be a devout man. Certainly Bishopscourt's appearance accords with a military role, particularly as the old tower used to be surrounded by a moat, parts of which can still be traced. The story goes that the bishop was allocated the landward-facing half of the tower, while the king retained the half facing the sea. No documentary evidence appears to exist to confirm the tale however. The earliest record of the house makes no mention of the king and states that Bishop Simon (bishop 1226-1247) was in residence.

Consecrated by the Archbishop of Nidaros, Norway, Simon was the first bishop to be accepted by all branches of the church as the rightful Bishop of Sodor and Man. Famous for many religious reforms and enterprises, he is particularly remembered for building St German's Cathedral on St. Patrick's Isle. He also ensured that the Bishop of Sodor and Man received revenue from the Manx estates granted to him, revenue which previously had usually disappeared into the pockets of stewards. Such lands became known as the Bishop's Barony (see chapter 4).

As well as income from property Bishop Simon established the Bishop's Barony Courts and created laws and regulations to ensure that the bishop's revenue would be regularly collected. Two Barony Courts (see also chapter 4) dealing with all matters relating to the bishop's land were held each year in May and October, with at least a hundred people attending. Any changes of tenant had to be approved by the court and recorded, and rents and customs, i.e. payments in kind, were collected. The business was conducted in Manx and the records kept in Latin. Some

St German's Cathedral, inside Peel Castle, St Patrick's Isle. Built by Bishop Simon

courts were held at Bishopscourt, others at Peel, Braddan (at Ballaquirk, now Farmhill Manor just west of Douglas), Ballakilley, The Nunnery, Kirk Arbory and Castle Rushen. Barony Courts continued to be held until the mid-nineteenth century.

Back to politics

For about two hundred years, at the beginning of the last millennium, Mann was a kingdom in its own right. The machinations of its rulers are extremely involved, rivalling a modern soap opera for complexity. Nevertheless, no history of the Isle of Man can really be complete without looking at its period of kingship. Readers unable to face even a simplified version of invasion, betrayal, counter-invasion, blood, battles and sudden death should read the final two sentences of this chapter and turn, thankfully, to chapter 4.

Those of you who are prepared to canter through a brief history of the saga of Manx kings – here goes.

The extent of the kingdom of Mann and the Isles varied according to the various power struggles, but at different times encompassed Mann, the Hebrides, Orkney plus parts of Ireland and some of mainland Scotland. In addition the ruler was never allowed to forget that Norway expected to be treated as the overlord of the kings of Mann. In 1153, therefore, Godred acting as ambassador for his father King Olaf I, visited the Norwegian King Inge 'the Hunchback', grandson of Mann's previous king Magnus 'Barelegs'. While Godred was paying his respects in Norway, his three cousins, who had been raised in Ireland, arrived in Mann with a large band of warriors and demanded to be given half the island. Prompted perhaps by family feeling or natural magnanimity (or perhaps lacking the support of warriors who had accompanied his son) King Olaf didn't immediately send his nephews packing, but invited them to a parley. In the act of saluting the king with his axe, Reginald, the middle brother, cut off his uncle's head.

42

Dividing the Isle of Man between them, the three brothers immediately tried to emulate their grandfather Magnus by subjugating Galloway, but the Scots were having none of it and drove them away. In the meantime Godred, returning from Norway, was understandably angry about his father's assassination and landed in Orkney where 'all the chieftains of the Isles were overjoyed when they heard he had come, and at an assembly unanimously elected him their king.' It's interesting that the *Chronicles* use the Latin verb *elegere* (*eligere*), which means 'to choose', so the leaders of the island communities appear to elect their king, rather than Godred assuming the kingship by right of succession. Kings can of course become such simply because they have a bigger or more efficient fighting force than anyone else, but setting conquest aside, in the eleventh century there were two routes to rule. English and Scottish Kings gained their throne by hereditary rights, while Kings in Ireland were chosen by an assembly of leaders who at the same time appointed the king's successor in case of his sudden death. It sounds as though the King of Mann and the Isles was decided using some system similar to that of the Irish.

Once confirmed in post Godred lost no time in sailing to Mann and putting his father's killers to death. He seems, at least at first, to have been popular, as the people of Dublin sent an envoy to Mann requesting that Godred become their king also. Dublin was supposed to be under the rule of Muirchertach III, High King of Ireland, but Muirchertach was unable to oust Godred and the Manx, helped as they were by the Dubliners.

Godred's success seems to have gone to his head, for, as the Chronicles say, 'he began exercising tyranny against his chieftains, for some of them he disinherited, while others he deprived of their positions.' Those chieftains were the ones who had chosen Godred to be king, remember, and probably expected more in the way of gratitude. Thorfin, one of their number, decided to do the twelfth century equivalent of giving Godred the sack. Godred's father, Olaf, had had a number of illegitimate children, one of whom was married to Somerled, King of Argyll. Thorfin went to Somerled and asked that his son Dougal, i.e. Godred's nephew, come and rule Mann instead of his uncle. The *Chronicles* explain what happened next:

'Somerled was very much pleased to hear this request and handed his son Dougal over to him [Thorfin], who took and conducted him through all the Isles. He subjected them all to his sway and received hostages from each island. But one chieftain called Paul made a secret escape to Godred and told him everything that had taken place. Godred was alarmed to hear this and straightway ordered his men to prepare ships and to hasten to meet them. Somerled with his men collected a fleet of eighty ships and hastened to meet Godred.

'In the year 1156 a naval battle was fought on the night of the Epiphany between Godred and Somerled and there was much slaughter on both sides. When the day dawned they made peace and divided the kingdom of the Isles between them.' The division of the kingdom meant that Somerled took control of the islands Mull and Islay, which were closest to Argyll, while Godred retained control of Mann, Lewis and Skye. Somerled's holdings were therefore right in the middle of Godred's kingdom, like a thorn in the side.

The sea battle of 1156 wasn't the last encounter between the brothers-in-law. Two years later Somerled came again, defeated Godred, and sacked Mann. Godred fled to Norway leaving Somerled in possession of the island. The Argyll king left Mann, some say because of the intervention of St Maughold (see chapter 9), but also appears to have left a power vacuum. Godred did not return to Mann until 1164, but it's possible that the intervening six years saw Somerled's son Dougal govern the island on behalf of his father. That, after all, was what the leaders of the island peoples had asked for in the first place.

In 1164, after Somerled's death in battle at Renfrew on the Scottish mainland, Godred's illegitimate brother Reginald opportunely seized the Manx throne. He didn't have it long. Four days later Godred appeared with an army borrowed from Magnus V of Norway. By now Godred appears to have been fed up with the scheming of his relations as he blinded and castrated Reginald before resuming the throne. Godred ruled for another twenty-three years, dying on St Patrick's Isle on 10 November 1187. He is buried at the traditional burying place of the Kings of Mann and the Isles, at St Oran's Shrine on Iona.

Godred left three sons, Reginald, Olaf and Ivar, the first of whom was technically illegitimate, although his parents, Godred and Fionnula, granddaughter of a King of Ireland, had subsequently married. Godred had always intended that his heir should be Olaf, his second son, but the boy was only ten when his father died. Fearing that a regent would usurp the boy's powers, the Manx leaders established Reginald, his elder brother, as king. To put such thinking into context, the previous year, Ruaidri, the last High King of Ireland had been deposed by the English; Norway was undergoing a lengthy Civil War led by rival kings, Magnus V and Sverre; and Gwynedd in Wales was divided between David I, Rhodri II and Gruffydd III, two brothers and a nephew. The Manx were aiming to get an adult leader capable of keeping the peace of the realm for some time. Fine in theory, the decision unfortunately didn't work in practice.

Reginald had problems right from the start. Not only did his brother Olaf want what he considered his rightful place as King of Man, but the kings of Norway and England were both pressurising Reginald to help them with their separate designs on Ireland. Reginald kept his brother quiet for a time by giving him Lewis on which to live, but in 1208 when Olaf complained that farming was poor, Reginald had him arrested and asked William 'the Lion', King of Scotland to keep him locked up. Only when William died, seven years later, did Olaf return to Lewis. He and Reginald also returned to squabbling over the kingdom, occasionally supported or otherwise by such opportunists as Henry III of England, Alan, Lord of Galloway and Thomas, Earl of Athol. After fighting his brother's troops at Ronaldsway in 1226, Olaf ousted Reginald from the kingship of Mann in fact, if not in law. Two years later, at the Battle of Tynwald – a real battle, not a legal or political one – Olaf and the northern Manx fought Reginald and the southern Manx and Reginald was killed. Monks from Rushen Abbey conveyed the king's body to their mother church in Furness where, as the *Chronicles* say: 'he was buried in the place he had chose for himself while he was alive.'

Olaf II's reign was much more peaceful than that of his brother, not least because he had no rival brother contending with him; Ivar appears to have faded out of history somewhere in the previous forty years. Olaf did, however, have to exercise some political sleight of hand in order to reconcile various expedient allegiances. The Norwegian civil war was finally over and Norway's sea strength growing again so Olaf had to be mindful of the old tribute. Against that, England, whose power had been growing for some time, now held much of Ireland, and the English King Henry III persuaded Olaf to help defend the English and Irish coastline around the Irish Sea. There were skirmishes, not least from pirates raiding Mann for the pickings. Despite being squeezed by his powerful neighbours, Olaf II's reign was the closest thing to peace the island had known for many years. He died on St Patrick's Isle in 1237 and was buried in Rushen Abbey.

Harald, Olaf's son, was only fourteen when he came to the throne, but, born at the height of Olaf's strife with his brother Reginald, Harald seems to have remembered and learned from the political chicanery going on during his formative years. Apart from a violent spat at a meeting of Tynwald in 1237, during which representatives of the king were killed, Harald's reign was largely peaceful. Once again the question of acknowledging Norway's supremacy came up and Harald was inclined to ignore it. Since the end of the Norwegian civil war, however, co-regents

Haaken IV 'the Elder' and his son Haaken 'the Younger' were stronger and less preoccupied. The year after Harald's succession the two Haakens sent Gospatrick and Gilchrist to Mann to remind the young king of his manners. As the *Chronicles* say: 'They expelled Harald from the kingdom of Mann, because he refused to go to the court of the king of Norway. They took over the governorship of the whole country and collected the king's dues for the use of the king of Norway.' It was four more years before the Norwegian king ratified Harald as King of Mann and the Isles. The young king, now nineteen, was only allowed to return to Mann in 1242.

In 1247 Harald again left Mann, visited England where he was knighted by King Henry, and travelled to Norway, this time to marry the Norwegian king's daughter. Either the nuptial celebrations were particularly extensive, or there was much to discuss, as Harald spent more than a year in Norway, only sailing for Mann in the autumn of 1249. He never arrived. A violent storm blew up off the coast of Shetland and he, his new family, Laurence the new Bishop of Sodor and Mann, and his entire retinue were drowned.

The loss at the same time of so many of the nobility of Mann and the Isles created another power vacuum, and the kingdom suffered four kings in three years, none of whom had the backing of the Norwegian king. Eventually, in 1252, Magnus, the youngest son of Olaf II, was crowned king in Mann. Incidentally, it was probably Magnus who founded Castle Rushen at around this time. One year later, he was confirmed as King of Mann and the Isles by Haaken IV of Norway. There was trouble in the wings however.

Magnus was King of Mann and the Isles, and it was the 'isles' part of his kingdom which rankled with his neighbours. Almost exactly one hundred years earlier remember, the kingdom had been divided when the King of Argyll had taken control of Mull and Islay, leaving Lewis and Skye to the King of Mann. Mull and Islay had descended to the Scottish kings, who were eager to take over the whole of the Hebrides and felt that they had a good chance of keeping them once obtained, as the islands were closer to the Scottish mainland than they were to Mann. Alexander II of Scotland had first mooted the idea to Haaken IV of Norway, the overlord of the King of Mann, but died before the issue could be resolved. His son, Alexander III, continued with the negotiations but wearied of them and opted instead for open hostilities.

In 1263 the kings of Norway and Scotland fought for possession of Lewis and Skye. The Norwegians were defeated more by the weather than the Scots, and Haaken IV died on his way home. Without his overlord Magnus had no chance of keeping the isles part of his kingdom, and without the good will of the king of Scotland, not much of retaining the throne of Mann itself. The allegiance formerly owed to Norway was hastily transferred to Scotland, and Magnus also promised to supply his new overlord with ten war galleys as often as he need them. In return, from being the King of Mann and the Isles, Magnus agreed to become the King of Mann only. Two years later he was dead. In 1265 Magnus died at Castle Rushen and was buried in the Abbey of St Mary at Rushen. The following year Magnus VI 'the Law Mender', King of Norway effectively sold the entire kingdom of Mann and the Isles to Alexander III of Scotland for four thousand marks. Nearly five hundred years after the Vikings first invaded, the Manx independent kingdom, and the island's long allegiance to Norway was over.

CHAPTER 4

THE SCOTS, THE ENGLISH AND THE LORDS OF MANN

During the period of Norse rule, the island's symbol, not surprisingly, was a Viking ship. The three legs of Mann seem to have replaced the ship around 1266 when Alexander III of Scotland gained control of the island, although both symbols may have been used earlier and continued to be used concurrently for a while. No-one really knows the

origination of the three legs of Mann, but the emblem appears to be an amalgam of two and possibly three separate symbols.

Magnus III, the last King of Norway also to style himself King of Mann, had as his shield device a mailed leg, bent at the knee with the toe pointing to the left when viewed. If the mailed leg possibly stems from Norway, the idea of using three together in a triskelion seems to have been copied or adapted from the Sicilian flag which has three naked legs with a face superimposed where the legs join. The connexion sounds a little far-fetched until you realise that Alexander III's wife was sister to the King of Sicily. The idea for the combination may have been assisted

The old symbol of the Isle of Man was a Viking ship; this is a stained glass window at Lonan Old Church

by Alexander III's own coat of arms, which is dominated by a large Y, again suggesting three 'legs'. The triskelion itself is an adaptation of an ancient symbol representing the sun.

New rulers, new rules

Much of the 150 years or so from the beginning of the Scottish rule of Mann until the elevation of the Stanley family to the role of the Lords of Mann is marked by wars between Scotland and England. Its strategic importance in the middle of the Irish sea, not only made the island a useful springboard for invasion north or south, but also allowed its ruler to dominate trade routes to Ireland. Mann was therefore often unable to avoid being dragged in to what was, after all, someone else's problem.

The powers that be might have decided that from 1266 the Isle of Man would belong to the Scots, but that didn't mean that the Manx people endorsed the decision. Rather like the employees of a firm on the receiving end of a hostile takeover, the Manx felt that their new rulers neither understood nor appreciated their laws, social organisation or way of life, and that the Scots considered the Manx to be very much second

Sicilian flag. Its similarity to the Manx 'three legs' emblem is obvious

Three legs of Mann in a shield on the Maughold cross now inside the church. With the exception of the Manx Sword of State, this is probably the earliest known representation of the three legs emblem

class. Almost the first thing Alexander III did with his new dominion was to appoint bailiffs to tax the Manx people. Although very little is known about actual events, it is reasonable to suppose that the foreign bailiffs of a successful king who had paid good money for his new territory, would have little compunction about making harsh demands on the indigenous population. Alexander and his bailiffs would have been unusual conquerors indeed if they had not tried to extract at least its purchase price from Scotland's new acquisition.

Godred, son of Magnus IV, the last King of Mann, was the natural leader of the growing discontent, and passive reluctance gradually turned into active resistance. After ten years of probably escalating violence, the Manx openly rebelled and in 1275 Alexander sent troops to quash the recalcitrant islanders. Led by John de Vescy, a disaffected Englishman from Alnwick but working as what amounted to a mercenary for the Scottish King, troops landed on St Michael's island, now linked to Langness but then a separate small island. Vescy sent an embassy to the local force to sue for peace, but Godred defied it. Before dawn Scottish troops landed on the Manx mainland at Ronaldsway and put down the Manx rebellion. Godred was killed, the last of the Norsemen to claim the Manx throne. The Scots remained in charge.

When Alexander III died in 1286 he was succeeded by his three-year-old granddaughter Margaret. She was known as the Maid of Norway as, although her mother was Alexander's daughter Margaret, her father was the Norwegian king Eirik II. As was usual in mediaeval courts when a successor was a minor – and a girl at that – other leaders began to consider how much a crown would suit them. The death of Margaret, aged only seven and after only four years, led to a number of claimants for the Scottish throne. Scotland itself was torn apart by internal wrangling and the Isle of Man, further away and more difficult to defend but yet of strategic importance, was again considered a prize for whoever could take and hold it. The most powerful ruler in the surrounding islands was Edward I of England. Edward had always regarded the Isle of Man as properly belonging to England but had not yet had time to make good his claim. He did so now.

Although officially ruled by the kings of England, English rule in Mann at the end of the thirteenth century was patchy at best. The island was a long way from the centre of power in England and, with the English monarch also laying claim to large areas of France, English kings typically looked south to Europe for the expansion of their kingdom. On the other hand the small island almost off the edge of his map was of great strategic value and Edward II

in particular never overlooked it. The English king used Manx seamen and Manx supplies in his war against Scotland, and several times warned his bailiffs against allowing any injury to be committed against his faithful subjects on the Isle of Man. The Manx were divided in their loyalties however, or, more likely, were canny enough to exploit rulers who were none of their choosing.

While some of the Manx were victualling Edward's ships, others supported Robert I ('the Bruce'), King of Scotland, in his attacks against England. On 18 May 1313 Robert landed at Ramsey and spent the night at Douglas Priory, now called The Nunnery. The Bruce then laid siege to Castle Rushen which Lord Dougal Mac Dowyl was holding for Edward II. In December the castle fell and Mann reverted to Scottish rule under Robert's nephew Thomas Randolph, Earl of Moray. For years afterwards, regardless of who was officially supposed to be ruling Mann, the descendants of the Earls of Moray used the three legs of Mann device and title King of Man whenever it suited them.

St Michael's Island. Once a separate island but now linked to Langness by a narrow causeway

Robert the Bruce used the Isle of Man as a handy base for invading Ireland and, in 1316, perhaps in retaliation Richard le Mandvil and his brothers landed at Ronaldsway from Ireland with the intention of conquering Mann. Incidentally, the landing of Irish troops on what was the wrong side of Mann from Ireland might need some explanation. For many years Ronaldsway was one of the island's major harbours, well sheltered from the prevailing westerlies and protected to seaward by the Langness peninsular. It was one of the reasons that Castle Rushen was built where it was. Unfortunately Ronaldsway experiences tricky currents and dries out at low tide, so other harbours gradually became preferred.

Battle was fought between the Scots and Irish near South Barrule and the Manx fled, possibly considering that the Scottish king's troubles were nothing to do with them. The final entry in the Manx *Chronicles* reads: 'They [the Irish] plundered the land of all its more valuable produce… After this they came to Rushen Abbey and plundered it so extensively of its furniture, cattle and sheep,

The site of the Battle of Ronaldsway. Troops sent by Alexander III of Scotland landed here in 1275 and quashed the Manx rebellion. Ronaldsway Farm is surrounded by aerodrome buildings

A Brief History of the Isle of Man

The Nunnery. Formerly the home of the Goldie-Taubman family it is now the site of the Isle of Man University College, part of Liverpool John Moores University

that they left nothing at all. And when they had spent a month at such activities they loaded their ships up with the more valuable assets of the country and in this way returned home.'

Over the next thirteen years the Scottish and English kings both claimed the island and invaded it in turn. The ordinary Manx people must have become adept at hiding their animals and goods or there would have been nothing left for them to live on. The question of the island's ruler was not settled until the English King Edward III ordered the invasion and capture of Mann in 1329. From then on Mann was inextricably tied to England.

Isolated or cosmopolitan?

The political musical chairs made life difficult for the ordinary Manx people, as each new ruler tended to want to squeeze the island for all they could get out of it. Like almost all countries at this time, the Manx economy was land-based, i.e. reliant on agricultural production. The island was however more of an amorphous amalgam of the social organisation of its various invaders than the more rigid feudal system which dominated most of mediaeval society in England and Scotland. To start with, the island still had the remnants of Norse organisation and way of life and its five-hundred-year history of *things* (see chapter 3) regulated the laws of the land. Literally the land, as in the thirteenth century, land was what provided people with most of the means to survive. The mediaeval England and Scotland of the island's squabbling rulers may have had a strip-field system worked by serfs and owing allegiance to the lord of the manor, but such was not Mann's experience.

Few ordinary people in Europe had the traditional independence and freedom of movement (via the sea) of the Manx. Today it's difficult to appreciate just how important the sea was as a means of communication. It's only very very recently, almost within the last few decades and certainly within the last hundred years, that people wishing to move themselves or their goods tend to consider road, rail or air travel first. Up until as recently as the 1960s scheduled passenger ships circled the British Isles and were regularly used as the best means of getting from the south of England to Scotland. For centuries the sea had been busy with small ships bustling round the coastline between ports or butting across the Irish Sea, collecting and delivering cargoes and passengers. The Isle of Man was at the hub of most of the major communication and trade routes between Ireland, Wales, England and Scotland and near the coastal shipping routes. Nothing which could go by water was carried by land, and the island offered a convenient stopping-off point in the centre of a sea criss-crossed by trading vessels. In the fourteenth century, Mann was about as isolated as Gatwick Airport.

The ease of seaboard communication, as least compared with overland routes, meant that wealth, previously centred on ownership of land, began to be generated more and more by trade. Merchants grew richer and, in growing richer, grew more powerful. Many luxury goods came from Europe, but the English also purchased items such as waterproof clothing from Ireland. Their country's higher rainfall meant that the Irish had become adept at fashioning hooded woollen cloaks which were impervious to everything except a deluge. It rained a lot in England too and the Irish cloaks were popular, if expensive. Other goods and animals such as horses were also traded. The Isle of Man was excellently placed to take advantage of any lucrative trade crossing the Irish Sea, as well as finding outlets for its own surplus goods.

The geography of Mann doesn't lend itself easily to the creation of roads, and wheeled traffic was unknown until the eighteenth century (see chapter 5). Wherever possible, goods for trading or other bulky items were carried by water, often the sea but sometimes by the larger rivers. Sometimes water transport was not possible and in these cases goods were carried by chapman (a man carrying a pack) or pack animal on trackways created by feet and custom. Some mediaeval pack horse roads still exist, such as the one running from Laxey harbour up Old Laxey Hill to the south, and to the north over the old bridge and up Breeze Hill. The old pack horse route is still known as Puncheon Road or Laxey Old Road and was once the only way into the old village of Laxey except by sea. Possibly the most famous of such ancient trackways is known as the Royal

The track is Laxey Old Road. Once the only route into the fishing village of old Laxey, the vertical road clearly visible on the hill opposite is Old Laxey Hill and marks where the track continued towards Douglas

A Brief History of the Isle of Man

Way and stretches from Ramsey to Castletown; the Millennium Way long distance footpath is based on it.

For those loads which were just too large to carry, but where water was not available, the Manx may have used sledges which ran on grass. These were fairly common in Ireland, where they were known in Irish Gaelic as *carrs*. Designed to run well on turf and peat, carrs may have been used to transport loads inland on the Isle of Man, particularly on the grassy, unwooded slopes of the island's uplands.

Multi-skilled

The ordinary Manx people were farmers, fishers and traders from choice, warriors from necessity. The various rulers who claimed Mann usually backed up their claim by invasion, pillage and/or taxation, thus robbing the Manx people of food and stores. Partly from the depredations of their new overlords and partly because of the size of the property, farms would not often support an entire family. Some of the men would spend part of their time working elsewhere to bolster the family income while the women kept things going at home and did much of the work on the farm. Seafaring – either fishing or working on trading vessels – and mining were the two most common sources of extra income. Menfolk returning after a period of work would have been bound to talk over with their families the strange things they had seen and the people they'd met. Peasants from the larger islands surrounding Mann would not

Old postcard of Ireland showing carr. Similar sledge-like vehicles were used on Mann and can occasionally be seen in use at Cregneash

have had such experience of other peoples and so were far more isolated by comparison.

The island's position, surrounded by larger often hostile countries, probably meant that the Manx were to a certain extent multi-lingual, rather like the Dutch today. Manx, Irish and Scottish Gaelic are part of the goidelic group of Celtic languages while Welsh, Cornish and Breton make up the brythonic group. The differences between the two groups stem from the relationship between the tribes of the original Viking invaders. Even so, during the thirteenth and fourteenth centuries the Gaelic languages would probably have been similar enough for the peoples to have been able to communicate with each other; even today the Gaelic of different areas is very similar. Up until the middle of the fourteenth century French remained the official language of England, although English was growing in ascendancy and widely spoken; it replaced French as the national language of England in 1362. The church meanwhile conducted its services and kept its records in Latin.

Manx merchants would probably have had smatterings of French and English, plus Scottish and Irish Gaelic where it differed from Manx and may in addition have been able to get by in Welsh and Cornish. They, or more probably their clerks, may also have been familiar with Latin. Manx fishermen would be able to make themselves understood in the ports of most of the countries surrounding Mann and also probably those in Scandinavia, as bad weather would force them to take shelter in various harbours. Their wives would speak only Manx, and so would their children, taught at home by the women of the family.

Its seafaring contact with the wider world meant that Mann was not as quarantined from disease as might have been expected. Its ports offered shelter to traders not only from the neighbouring islands, but also to Scandinavian and occasionally Mediterranean ships. Outside the port areas, however, most of the Manx people lived in small agricultural communities, which restricted the spread of epidemic. Each community had little daily contact with its neighbours and, with springs running off the hills, usually had a clean water supply. From 1348 to 1350 between a third and half the population of Britain died of bubonic plague. Diseases such as plague and measles need high densities of population to spread quickly, as the bacteria, although virulent, are not long lived. The sparse and widely-scattered Manx population would not have been a good breeding ground for disease, so would probably have been naturally healthy, although often hungry. There is no record of plague reaching Mann, but it may have done so and yet not caused high numbers of deaths;

Mining became more common during the later centuries as technology made deep mining possible, but extracting ore from the ground had been a feature of island life and something of a cottage industry since the Iron Age (see chapter 2). The Abbot of Furness Abbey, the mother house of Rushen Abbey, had been granted mineral rights on Mann in 1246 by King Harald;

Model of Rushen Abbey at the Rushen Abbey site,
showing how it might have looked in its heyday

A Brief History of the Isle of Man

remains dating from the thirteenth or fourteenth century of what was probably a bowl hearth for smelting or refining iron have been found at Kirk Braddan; and Edward I of England granted John Comyn, 3rd Earl or Mormaer (a regional or provincial ruler in mediaeval Scotland) of Buchan a licence to dig lead on the Calf of Man. The earl wanted a new roof for his castle at Cruggleton in Galloway. He might have been granted the licence, but it was Manxmen who did the digging.

The quiet power

Amid the hurly burly of invasion and counter invasion, buying and selling, political wrangling and the search for fortunes, the church with its emphasis on a simple contemplative life might have been thought to have provided a sharp contrast with the secular world. Such was not the case.

Rushen Abbey was a daughter house of the Cistercian foundation of Furness (see chapter 3), and the Cistercians were one of the wealthiest of the monastic orders. Unlike Benedictines who regularly built monasteries in or near towns, the phrase often quoted from the Cistercian rule is that their houses be founded 'far from the concourse of men', and usually in low-lying land beside running water. Great importance was placed on manual, particularly agricultural, labour in order to become self-sufficient. However the Cistercians realised that monks could not participate in a full liturgical day and also do sufficient work to provide for the needs of the community. They therefore introduced the concept of lay-brothers who were primarily responsible for managing the land and animals, yet observed the rules of the order and took vows of obedience.

By the fourteenth century the Cistercians had what amounted to a two-tier membership.

Lay brothers and monks not only formed separate but complementary communities within the abbey, but were seen as distinct vocations. Lay brothers were not trainee monks – and indeed were not allowed to be – but servants of the abbey in their own sphere. Both communities worked and prayed, but the monks' life centred around the church services, while that of the lay brothers centred on their labour. Monks were literate, lay brothers were not. Inevitably the monks were drawn from a much wider area, often from the mother house or other daughter houses overseas. Lay brothers would almost always have been indigenous Manx.

Lay brothers were essential to Rushen Abbey to help it manage its increasingly large land holding. The abbey owned almost half the land in Malew parish where it was situated, about a fifth of that in German stretching from Peel eastwards, a large chunk of the middle of Lezayre west of Ramsey, and smaller parcels of land in Rushen, Lonan and Maughold. The amount of land owned by the various branches of the church grew hugely in the fourteenth and fifteenth centuries with Douglas Priory, Whithorn Priory, St Bees Priory, Bemaken Friary, Bangor Abbey and Sabal Abbey all holding land on Mann.

Whether driven by their aim to distance themselves from the secular world, or by sheer necessity, the Cistercians developed a new way of managing their property. Rather than introducing to Mann the type of feudal relationship which was the case throughout most of Britain, Rushen Abbey established self-contained grange farms of the type normal among Cistercian houses and which acted as centres of agriculture. Bellabbey Farm near Colby in Arbory is said to have been one of the grange farms for Rushen Abbey. The Cistercians were noted for operating the mediaeval equivalent of intensive farming. Even their critics acknowledged that they were excellent farmers and developed the most out of even unlikely sites. Cistercians were skilled at draining land, they shaped stone and used it for building and were adept at channelling and harnessing running water. Their craftsmanship, coupled with their new methods of farming, changed the landscape.

Involved in both arable and pastoral farming, the Cistercians were particularly renowned as major wool-growers. Throughout Europe they were known not only for the quantity of wool they produced, but also for the innovative changes they made to the way the wool was farmed, sold and traded. The monks became merchants and Furness Abbey became the second richest Cistercian house in England – the richest was Fountains Abbey in Yorkshire – with its own fleet of trading ships. Rushen Abbey, its daughter house, would have been part of a large-scale enterprise, regularly visited by the Furness Abbey ships to collect Manx goods for trading and bring whatever the monks needed or their neighbours could buy.

Baronial bravura

The ecclesiastical lands on the Isle of Man formed different civil jurisdictions known as baronies. There were two types of baron. The older titles held their barony by tenure and, by the end of the thirteenth century, newer titles were granted their barony by writ. In other words barons could become known as barons simply because they had held their land for a long time, or they could be granted the title by the king. As all the barons on Mann were ecclesiastical barons, they had been granted their lands by the king and so were barons by writ. There were eight of them: the Abbot of Rushen Abbey, the Abbot of Furness in Cumbria, the Prioress of the Nunnery at Douglas, the Prior of Whitehorn in Galloway, the Abbot of Bangor in Northern Ireland, the Abbot of Sabal also in Northern Ireland, the Prior of St Bees in Cumberland and the Bishop of Sodor and Man. Bishop Richard who died in 1274 is usually accepted as the first Baron bishop. The distinction between barony by tenure and barony by writ made little difference during the thirteenth and fourteenth centuries, but became much more important when the monasteries were dissolved.

A barony was an administrative division of land, the owner of which had manorial rights. They included mineral and timber rights, the right to hunt animals and birds, the right to take fish from rivers, the right to insist that tenants used only the lord's mill, and the right to control the use of common and unenclosed land. To enforce his rights the baron could hold a manorial court at which infringements of manorial rights were punished and relations between tenants regulated. There were two main types of manor court, the court baron and court leet, usually presided over by a steward. The former dealt largely with the estate and its regulation while the latter had a wider remit covering public order and minor criminality. The Abbot of Rushen Abbey and the Bishop of Sodor and Man each had both.

Courts met regularly, at least every half year and sometimes as frequently as every three weeks. Many of the offences brought before the manorial court of Rushen Abbey were subject to a fine, but some carried the death penalty. The abbot's gallows were situated on Black Hill, north east of the abbey, and he may have had others in other parts of the island. When the monks built the packhorse bridge across the Silverburn River in around 1350 it not only provided easier access to abbey's estates on the other side of the river, but also to the abbot's gallows.

Monk's Bridge, near Rushen Abbey. Is was probably constructed by lay brothers to provide dry access to monastic lands, and for trading purposes

of the river, but also to the abbot's gallows. Barony Courts continued to be held regularly until the mid-nineteenth century. Only Manx Gaelic was used to conduct the business, although the records were kept in Latin. The last one was held in 1916 in the Barony of Bangor and Sabal, which is between Dalby and Glen May.

Priests, parishes and prelates

The monastic arm of the church was largely separate from its diocesan brethren, and there was much rivalry between the two, particularly when it came to the collection of tithes. Parishes had been introduced probably around 1275 and probably from England via Scotland. Manx parishes differ enormously from those in England however, and hearken back to the old system of keills (see chapter 3). Parish churches tended to grow out of keills, or it might be more accurate to say that certain keills were newly elevated and labelled as parish churches. However keills were usually built to provide for the spiritual wellbeing of isolated farming communities and therefore almost invariably built on isolated sites in farmland often near the coast. Consequently the English pattern of cottages and pub clustered around their parish

Castle Rushen. Probably founded by Magnus IV c. 1252, but rebuilt extensively around 100 years later

church and the whole clinging onto the skirts of a great house somewhere in the vicinity, is almost never seen on Mann. Parishes on the island are much more likely be scattered farming communities, and/or groups of houses, situated quite separately from the parish church which serves them.

With archbishops in Norway and England and the leader of the Cistercian order in France all claiming the right to consecrate the Bishop of Sodor and Man (see chapter 3), exactly whose bishop was successful tended to depend on who ruled the island at the time and who his friends were. After Alexander III of Scotland conquered Mann in 1266 new bishops were consecrated in Norway by the Archbishop of Nidaros, now Trondheim. They tended to be Scottish. Once the English under Sir William Montacute got possession of the island in 1334 the Norwegian archbishop fell out of favour and future bishops tended to be confirmed in post in Europe, although not necessarily in Britain. When Thomas de Rossy died in 1348, for example, William Russell appears to have been elected (unanimously!) by the clergy of his diocese. Rather unusually for positions of authority on the island at the time, William was a Manxman and had been Abbot of Rushen Abbey for eighteen years. He was confirmed as bishop by Bertrand du Pouget, Cardinal-bishop of Ostia in 1348.

Pope Clement VI agreed to William's appointment – the technical term is 'provided him' – but made it clear that he still considered the bishopric subject to Nidaros. The Cistercians were almost certainly delighted to be getting one of their own in post, the Pope's letter probably pacified the Norwegian archbishop, and no-one seems to have considered what the Archbishop of York thought about it.

Unless Mann was actually under threat of invasion the island's nominal rulers tended to have other things to think about, so little was done to check the might of the church on the island. Bishops passed their own laws and, unlike the secular law of the time, wrote them

A Brief History of the Isle of Man

down. Records from the synod held by Bishop Mark in 1291, for example, stated that: 'Under pain of excommunication, we ordain that all persons in our diocese pay tithes of all their goods…namely, of every kind of blade, of pulse, of swine, and of fruits, whether growing in gardens or in fields.' Tithes were also to be paid on animals, fish, dairy produce, woven and metal goods and the profits of trade, whether made by Manxmen or those based elsewhere and merely offloading some cargo in port.

In 1299, in an effort to check the growing demands of the church, Edward I expelled Bishop Mark from the island. Pope Boniface VIII came to the aid of his exiled bishop and placed the diocese, which of course meant the whole of Mann, under an interdict for three years. This effectively meant that only baptism and last rites were allowed; all sacraments such as marriage and mass were forbidden. The political power struggle went on for three years, the English King tried persuasion, the Pope held firm and the Manx people suffered.

Victory by Boniface meant that Bishop Mark returned to Mann in 1302. To flaunt his authority and perhaps inflict his own punishment on the people who had dared to question it, the bishop imposed a tax of one penny per year on every house with a fireplace. The 'smoke penny' wasn't unique to Mann but was a recognised episcopal tax also levied in Wales, the English lake district and various English counties. It was said to be a payment in lieu of a tithe of the wood burned for warmth and cooking. The Manx paid it for centuries.

The political machinations between England and Scotland in the early fourteenth century also affected the church as they disrupted the training and availability of priests; an English diocese would not employ clergy from a country with which they were at war. Those available tended to be directed to posts considered more important and possibly more comfortable. In 1350 or 1351 Bishop William held a synod at Kirk Michael ostensibly to increase the number of clergy on the island. Priests were recruited from Ireland, but neither of sufficient quality nor quantity. And the clergy at this time were also responsible for what little education was available. Ten years later Bishop William was still worrying about the paucity of priests when, in 1362, he complained to Pope Urban V that the wars between England and Scotland had reduced the number of available clergy. He was having problems finding educated churchmen who were able to combine the knowledge of Latin necessary to celebrate the church services with the ability to speak Manx to communicate with their congregations. As a result the pope gave the bishop permission to appoint to the priesthood eight 'illiterates', i.e. men unable to read or speak Latin.

During the 1350/1 synod at Kirk Michael, Bishop William is also thought to have required his priests to teach their congregations the Apostles' Creed in Manx. The creed is the oldest in the Christian church, written in the first or second century (although not by the apostles) and lays down the bedrock of the Christian faith. It begins 'I believe in God the Father Almighty, Maker of heaven and earth…' In Manx it is '*Ta mee credjal ayns Jee yn Ayr Ooilley-niartal, Chroo niau as thalloo…*' The Apostles' Creed still forms part of Morning and Evening prayer in Christian churches today. Bishop William could not, however, have left such a seminal tenet of the faith to translations which were random, differing and possibly inaccurate, particularly as he was having trouble finding bi-lingual (Latin-Manx) clergy. If his requirement is true, he must surely have provided an accredited translation for his priests to use. It would be the earliest recorded translation of part of the liturgy into Manx. It's a pity it no longer survives.

The island gets a king again
Five years after English King Edward III ordered the invasion and capture of Mann in 1329 (see above) he granted the right to rule it to one of his best supporters, William Montacute, 1st

Earl of Salisbury. When the king did so he probably had little thought of resurrecting the old idea of Mann as an independent kingdom, particularly as he had just spent over a decade trying to gain and regain Mann for the English throne. Edward was much more likely to be willing to sign over the troublesome island to a loyal supporter, in return for security against ambitious northern kings; the Earl had a fearsome reputation as a fighter and strategist. On 9 August 1334, the king himself penned the letter that granted Montacute the lordship of Mann: 'Know that…we have remitted and released, and entirely for us and for our heirs quitted claim, to our beloved and faithful William de Monte Acuto, all our right and claim which we have had, or in any manner can have, to the Island of Man, with its appurtenances whatsoever.' Montacute and his descendents were appointed absolute rulers of the island. Two years later the Earl was also appointed Admiral of the Fleet from the mouth of the Thames westward, presumably including the western coastline of England and the Irish Sea.

Mann's new ruler spent little time there as his duties to Edward III and, from 1377, to Richard II meant that he travelled all over Europe. He did however make at least one decision which influenced Mann for centuries to come. He rebuilt and expanded Castle Rushen, which had been destroyed by Robert the Bruce in 1313. It still remains one of the largest unruined buildings on the island. Some of the original keep was left standing and Montacute, or rather his Manx workmen, possibly reinforced by labour from Wales, repaired it, before going on to build most of the edifice within the curtain wall, plus the wall itself. Local carboniferous limestone was used, probably from Scarlett quarry, and the huge building must have shone white and imposing across the small huddle of buildings which was Ronaldsway at the time.

So extensive was the rebuilding that William Montacute, who died in 1344, may not have seen it finished. After his death – from bruises gained in a joust at Windsor, which sounds

as though they disguised internal injuries – his son, also William, inherited the Manx crown. A fighter like his father, he appears to have had neither sensitivity nor finesse. In 1362, Bishop William of Sodor and Mann complained to the pope that St German's cathedral at Peel was being used as merely another building in the fortress which was St Patrick's Isle. In response Montacute seems to have vacated the cathedral, but also seems to have taken umbrage. For well over one thousand years Peel, or more particularly St Patrick's Island, had

Castle Rushen, inside the curtain walls. Much of the castle visible today was built by William Montacute, 1st Earl of Salisbury

A Brief History of the Isle of Man

been seen as the place of most importance on Mann. Montacute named his other castle, Castle Rushen, as his principal residence on the island, effectively moving his capital city east and south.

William Montacute the younger reigned in Mann for forty-nine years, although he spent most of his time fighting for his king against France and Scotland. During his reign Mann was at least relatively peaceful and could recover from the ravages of the constant invasions. He was obviously disinterested in an island so far from his main concerns however as, in 1393, it was sold for the second time. Richard le Scrope of Bolton Castle in England bought Mann for his son William for £10,000, an enormous sum in the fourteenth century. Capgrave in his *Chronicles of England* states: 'Sir William Scrop boute the ylde of Eubony, with the crowne, of Sir William Mountagu erl of Salesbury: for he that is Lord of this yle may were a crowne.

This yle stant betwixt Yngland and Yiland. The name is now Ile of Man.' Early writers, particularly those from Ireland, occasionally referred to Mann as Eumonia or Eubonia.

As well as being King of Mann, William le Scrope was Chamberlain of Ireland, governor of various castles, Knight of the Garter, Lord Chamberlain and eventually created 1st Earl of Wiltshire. He was absolutely loyal to Richard II of England and was trusted in return. In 1398, when Richard II banished Thomas Beauchamp, Earl of Warwick and one of the five English magnates known as the Lords Appellant, the king banished him to the Isle of Man, knowing that he would not be summarily released. William le Scrope and his brother Stephen were personally entrusted with transporting the earl to Mann, and ensuring that he stayed there. Beauchamp and his wife Margaret were imprisoned in Peel Castle, and the tower where they were thought to be held is still called the Warwick Tower in their honour.

Richard II banished the Warwicks for life, but their stay on the island lasted only about a year. Richard himself was deposed

Warwick Tower on the seaward side of Peel Castle

in 1399, and his successor, Henry IV, released Warwick and restored him his lands and titles. The new king also beheaded Richard II's loyal servant William le Scrope.

The death of le Scrope meant that the crown of Mann lacked a head to wear it. On the occasion of his coronation in 1399, Henry IV granted the lordship of Mann to Henry Percy, 1st Earl of Northumberland. Under the splendidly titled 'Concession of the Isle of Man by Service of the Lancaster Sword' Henry states: 'We have given and granted, of our especial grace and certain knowledge, to the said earl of Northumberland… to have and to hold to the said earl and his heirs all the Islands, Castles, Peel, and lordship aforesaid, together with the royalties, regalities, franchises, liberties, sea-ports and everything truly and properly belonging to the same, homages, fealties, wardenships, marriages, reliefs, escheats, forfeitures, waifs, strays, courts baron, views of frankpledge, leets, hundreds, wapentakes, seawreck, mines of lead and iron, fairs, markets, free customs, meadows, pastures, woods, parks, chaces, lands, warrens, assarts, purprestures, highways, fisheries, mills, moors, marshes, turbaries, waters, pools, vineries, ways, passages, and commons, and every other the profits, commodities, emoluments and appurtenances whatsoever to the Island, Castle, Peel and lordship aforesaid, belonging or appertaining, together with the patronage of the bishopric of the said Island of Man, also knights' fees, advowsons and patronage of abbies, priories, hospitals, churches, vicarages, chapels, chantries and every other ecclesiastical benefices whatsoever to the said Island...' That it was listed didn't necessarily mean that whatever it was existed on the island. The new king was nothing if not comprehensive.

Since 1309 when they purchased it, the principal residence of the Percys had been Alnwick Castle, the place from which John de Vescy set out to put down the Manx rebellion a hundred years earlier. Alnwick's connexion with Mann was little less tenuous the second time around. Percy remained King of Mann for less than six years. In 1405 Percy supported the rebellion organised by Richard de Scrope, Archbishop of York and a distant relative of the previous wearer of the Manx crown. When the rebellion failed Percy fled to Scotland.

Perhaps in poetic justice Henry IV decided to reward one of those instrumental in defeating the rebellion with the lordship of Mann lost by Percy as a result of it. In 1405, therefore, the English king granted the lordship of Mann to Sir John Stanley. A letter from Henry himself dated 4 October 1405 said: '...we lately, by our letters patent, entrusted to our beloved and faithful John Stanley, Chevalier, the Castle, Peel, and dominion of Man, and all Islands and Dominions belonging to the said Island of Man, together with the royalties, regalities, franchises, and all other profits and commodities specified in our said letters for our benefit, safety, and security to keep it during our pleasure.'

In delivering the island to Sir John, the king jumped the gun slightly as Percy had not yet been attainted and so had not yet been deprived of the lordship. That fact was to cause the Stanley family problems two centuries later. Even so, the Stanleys and their family connexions remained the Lords of Mann for the next three and a half centuries.

Peel Castle, St Patrick's Isle. Now linked by a causeway to Peel, the island was once separate from the Manx mainland, and a stronghold of great political significance

CHAPTER 5

TWO AND A HALF CENTURIES OF STANLEYS

No one thought the Stanleys would rule Mann for upwards of three centuries, least of all Henry IV when he granted Sir John lordship in 1405. The Stanley rule was subject to only two interruptions. The first was as much a result of political manoeuvrings and sharp practice as anything else; the second reflected the revolution in England and the introduction of the Commonwealth. If the King of England was beheaded then it's hardly surprising that his subject Lord of Mann was similarly insecure in post.

Despite such interruptions however, the family's tenure on the island lasted from roughly the time of Agincourt to just before the American War of Independence; from before printing had been introduced to Britain to the publication of Gulliver's Travels; from the regular use of bread trenchers as plates almost to the manufacture of Wedgwood pottery. In Mann the Stanleys came to power when the ordinary Manx people had suffered from constant invasion but were still largely farmers and seafarers. When their lordship of Mann finally ended the Manx people were prosperous, politically astute and working towards independence.

The new rulers take charge

Initially the grant of kingship of Mann had been for Sir John's lifetime only, but in 1406 the king granted him the title in perpetuity on payment of two falcons and his loyalty. The Calendar of Patent Rolls dated 6 April 1406 says: 'Grant to John Stanley, knight, and his heirs and assigns, in lieu of a grant to him for life, surrendered to be cancelled, of the island, castle, peel and lordship of Man and all islands and lordships pertaining to the island, not exceeding the value of £400 yearly, to hold with royal rights, royalties, franchises, liberties, etc. by service of rendering to the King two falcons immediately after doing homage and to the King's heirs two falcons on the days of their coronations...'

The tribute of two falcons demanded of the Stanleys in payment for the Kingship of Mann. These are pictured on an information board next to Tynwald Hill

The gift could be a wry comment both on the crest of the Stanleys and the hierarchy of hawks. In 1385 Sir John Stanley had married Isabella de Lathom, the eldest daughter of a family with no male heirs. The Lathom family crest was the eagle and child, sometimes called the bird and bantling; from the marriage the Stanleys adopted the Lathom crest as their own. By the rules of falconry at the time, only the king could hunt with an eagle; lords flew peregrine falcons. Viewed in this light, the gift of two falcons asked of Sir John by Henry IV made it clear that, although King of Mann, Stanley was still subservient to the King of England. The falcon is still used as one of the supporters of the Manx civil coat of arms today.

The first Sir John never visited Mann, being taken up with his duties for Henry IV in Ireland, but does appear to have sent his son, also John, to act in his stead. When the second Sir John succeeded to the lordship of Mann in 1414 he seemed determined to maintain his contact with

Manx civil coat of arms. The falcon supporter comes from the Stanley crest while the raven was important in Norse mythology and refers back to the island's Viking past

the island. He visited Mann in 1417, 1422 and 1423, the last two occasions presiding over a meeting of Tynwald. Unlike today, Tynwald did not always meet at St John's (see also chapter 3). The Manx statute books, for example, say about the 1422 Tynwald: 'The Courte of all the Country is houlders at Kirke Michell, upon the hill of Reneurling, before our most doubtfull Lorde, Sr John Standley, by the grace of God, King of Man and Isles, the Tewsdaye next after the Feaste of St Barthioamew the Apostle, in the year of our Lord Jesus Christ, 1422.' 'Doubtful', at this time, had nothing to do with improbability, but meant rather 'to be feared'; the meaning survives today in 'redoubtable'.

It's generally agreed that, although the Manx laws existed long before the second Sir John took over the island, it was he who first had them written down. The earliest Manx statutes are dated from the 1422 Tynwald and the book which contains them goes on to inform Sir John about the Tynwald ceremonial. To take just one example: 'Upon the Hill of Tynwald sitt in a chaire covered with a royall cloath and cushions, and your visage unto the east, your swoard before you, houlden with the pointe up-wards…' Six hundred years later very little has changed (see appendix 3). The seating is as stated and the Manx Sword of State is still carried upright in front of the Lord of Man or their representative the Lieutenant Governor. The sword is thought to date from the early fifteenth century – the blade was replaced probably in the late fifteenth or early sixteenth century – and may have been the Sword borne before Sir John Stanley at the 1422 Tynwald. Ceremonial bearing-swords are usually much larger than swords designed for combat, and are blunt with rounded ends, possibly to prevent anyone being tempted to use them on the king as Reginald did his axe (see chapter 3). The sword was a symbol of status and authority, while the cruciform shape placed religion firmly in support of the secular authority.

The power of the church on the island was in fact enormous as so much Manx land was under its control. The church also had various advantages which the state lacked. It levied tithes, had its own courts with recorded laws and penalties – the secular rulers were only just beginning to write laws down – and, in the case of the monastic arm, had a huge number of unpaid workers labouring to increase its wealth. By comparison the state was badly funded and had only piecemeal organisation. John Stanley, the second of the family to rule, set about strengthening his rule and understood that he would not truly be King in Mann until the power of the spiritual barons had been curtailed.

Stanley identified that the church's power, rather like the island's emblem, stood on three legs. The church administered the sacraments, had its own laws, and was independently wealthy, often exporting Manx-created wealth to use elsewhere. Stanley would not interfere with the church's religious duties, but could and did stop canon law taking precedence over civil law. The right of sanctuary was abolished and the spiritual barons made responsible for

62

returning the sanctuary seeker to face justice. The church was also prevented from accepting important visitors unknown to the ruler of Mann or his representative, and was discouraged from removing wealth from the island except for trading purposes. The regulations were intended to curb the power of the senior clerics who often acted as though they were secular lords. The parochial clergy, who tended to be just as poor as the flock they served, and who occasionally were subjected to unreasonable demands or levies from their superiors, benefited almost as much as the laity from the restriction of the church's autonomy and fiscal demands.

The rise of the Keys

Even as early as 1417 the record of Manx laws refers to 'The Twenty Four', who today would be called the Keys, showing that the both the office and number were well established. Suggestions about the origin of the term 'Keys' vary from being a derivation of the Norse for 'chosen', or the Scottish Gaelic for 'tax' or Irish Gaelic for 'rent', to being the 'key personnel' on the island. At the end of the nineteenth century, Historian and Speaker of the House of Keys A.W. Moore believed that the term probably derived from the Manx for 'The Twenty Four', *Kiare-as-feed*, clumsily pronounced and then transcribed by a fifteenth century English clerk. For centuries Manx speakers continued to refer to their representatives by their number and not, if Moore was right, their English phonetic name.

The earliest records suggest that the Keys were there to represent the people, although they tended to be co-opted by the other Keys when a vacancy occurred in their ranks, rather than chosen directly by the people they were supposed to represent. They were also elected for life unless they resigned or were dismissed by the King of Mann. Anyone nominated for the post needed to be male, over twenty-one, and the owner of landed property – which effectively exempted many merchants whose wealth was in goods rather than land. The stipulation about wealth of course meant that most ordinary people were disqualified from being one of The Twenty Four. None of the Keys was paid, but they were exempt from certain services levied on their peers.

Probably the most senior office to which an ordinary Manxman could aspire was Captain of the Parish. The nomenclature for the post was in fact often 'Captain and Warden of the Day and Night Watch' and the holder was responsible for the raising and training of militia, and for maintaining the system of watch and ward. Watch and ward had been introduced by the Vikings and was a form of early warning system designed to give those living on the island time to organise defence against or retreat from invaders. A rota of men kept a form of look out or sentry duty day and night from high points in each parish to alert the island to possible attack from

Watch and ward stained glass, St George's Church, Douglas

the sea. So important was the watch considered that very few people were exempt from taking part. Of all the island parishes, only Marown has no sea border, so an efficient watch and ward would provide enough warning to evacuate women and children from vulnerable areas and organise militia defence. Watch and ward continued in a modified form up until after the Second World War. The post of Captain of the Parish still exists and, although it no longer carries quite such a marshal flavour, the oath each takes still requires them to undertake their duties 'for the good government of this isle and the due execution of the laws thereof.'

The Ayres from the Viking ship burial at Knock y Doonee. Prominent mounds such as this were often used to maintain watch and ward; this is thought to be the night watch post for Andreas. Note: the ship burial is on private land

Another post which existed earlier than the first statutes, but which is mentioned in them is that of Deemster. Again the name is an anglicised term, probably stemming from the verb to deem, i.e. to judge. The Manx for Deemster is *briw*, which is similar to Brehon, the Irish Gaelic name for a high-ranking judge. Brehon Law or *Fénechas* (the law of the free landworkers) existed in a reduced form in Ireland until the beginning of the seventeenth century, so may have influenced legal procedures on Mann in the early fifteenth.

A deemster was and is usually understood to be a judge, although deemsters had a much larger administrative and law-giving role than is usual for those pronouncing judgement. The term is almost unique to the Isle of Man, although Jersey also has deemsters, whose role differs from their Manx namesakes. Mann usually has two Deemsters, although there have occasionally been more; two was certainly the case for the early part of the Stanley reign.

Left to get on with it!

The second Sir John's interest in the island was not continued by his heirs and neither of the next two rulers of Mann visited it. From 1437 to 1507 the island was under the effectual rule of a series of governors assisted by the local Manx administration. During that time life for the ordinary people stabilised and in many respects was better than that in the rest of Britain.

A Brief History of the Isle of Man

The staple diet of the ordinary Manx people consisted of herring, oat cakes and, once introduced, potatoes, with water, milk or buttermilk to drink. A traditional Manx blessing is *palchey puddase as skeddan dy liooar* (potatoes in plenty and herring enough). Beer or ale was reserved for special occasions such as market day, as hops were not grown on the island and most of the limited cereal crop was reserved for food and fodder. Local beer, when it was brewed, was flavoured with herbs and known as *jough* although the word in Manx today tends to be used for a drink (unspecified); the modern Manx word for beer or ale is *lhune*. The Manx ate little in the way of meat, as agricultural animals were bred for their yields of wool and/or milk. Coney, although living on the island, were not yet common, mountain hare had not yet been introduced and there were no wild deer. Amateur hunting was largely restricted to sea birds; either the birds themselves or their eggs. Fish, particularly herring however, was readily obtainable. Luxury goods such as honey, eggs, surplus fruit etc., were often bartered with traders and shopkeepers for items such as soap which people needed but couldn't easily make themselves.

In many respects Manx employment laws mirrored much of what happens today, and were far less severe than the conditions of service across the water. Servants who fell sick had to be cared for by their employers for one month, after which, if not recovered, the cost of their care fell on their friends and family. Employees were not permitted to seek work with an alternative employer without giving a proper period of notice, but Deemsters could insist that labourers with wages owing be paid. No Manxman could be arrested for debt without a special warrant from the lord or governor, and could not be arbitrarily imprisoned without sentence being passed by a Deemster. 'Yarding' was disliked by employer and employed alike, as it meant that labourers could be requisitioned at any time to serve the lord and/or his chief officers, but those yarded had to be paid; they were not expected to work for free. Wages tended to be fixed by statute, which was a mixed blessing as, while an employer could not cheat his workers, neither could he easily reward them for good service.

Herring Gull egg in nest at Peel Castle. Sea birds and their eggs once formed part of the diet of the Manx people

Women were much better treated under Manx law than their sisters in England, possibly as a result of an Irish influence on Manx law. In Ireland women were considered the equal of men, could train in the legal or medical profession and own property in their own right. In England, high-born women were considered the property of their nearest kin or overlord and useful only for making marriage alliances; lowly-born women could occasionally be independent but were usually subject to husband, father or brother. On Mann a widow inherited half her husband's property on his death and, if her husband committed a crime, did not lose her half of the property in forfeits for him. The rape of a married woman carried the death penalty, but that of a single woman left the man's fate in her hands. The Deemster called to pass sentence would offer the woman a rope, a sword and a ring. Her choice determined whether the man was hanged with the rope, beheaded with the sword or married to her with the ring!

Such laws make life on Mann sound much easier than across the water but, although Manx laws were often less harsh, living conditions were more so. Houses were small, dark and usually sheltered both people and animals, the latter helping to heat the home. Temperatures in Britain were generally more extreme during the latter part of the fifteenth century. A series of severe winters and even the occasional sea freeze were punctuated by the occasional hot drought-ridden summer. Life must have been harsh on Mann as island residents needed a licence to leave.

From king to lord

After an absence of seventy years, the ruler of Mann again visited his island when, in 1507 Thomas Stanley visited to deal with local trouble. The island had not been entirely forgotten in the meantime but, apart from being heavily taxed, seems to have been used mainly as a dumping ground for noble undesirables. Presumably the powers that be thought the island remote enough for exiles not to pose a continuing threat, but near enough for their return not to take too long if required. It was also reassuringly far from that hotbed of plotting, continental Europe.

One notable exile, for example, was Eleanor Cobham, wife to Humphrey, Duke of Gloucester, who was the son, brother and uncle of the kings of England Henry IV, Henry V and Henry VI respectively. Not content with her high place at court, in 1446 Eleanor schemed to make her husband King Humphrey I, and was accused of using witchcraft to bring it about. Her lower-class helpers were put to death, but she was more leniently treated. Henry VI ordered the ruling Stanley, another Sir Thomas and the 1st Baron, to imprison Eleanor on the Isle of Man. It's thought that she was confined in Peel Castle, possibly in a crypt under the chancel of St German's cathedral, where she stayed until she died probably around five years later.

Above: Derbyhaven, named after the 2nd Earl of Derby who landed there in 1507 Left: Thomas Stanley, 2nd Earl of Derby landing at Derbyhaven in 1507, pictured on a commemorative stamp issued in 1982

From 1504 when he inherited the title, Thomas Stanley, the 2nd Earl of Derby generally and perhaps tactfully preferred the title Lord of Mann to that of King. Henry VII of England was this Stanley's overlord and notoriously suspicious of any apparent threat to his power. Nineteen years earlier, Henry had defeated and killed Richard III at the Battle of Bosworth to take the English throne. Being only the great grandson of the illegitimate son of the third son of Edward III, Henry had far less right to the throne than the man he defeated who had inherited the crown from his brother. And Richard only lost Bosworth because of the defection of

A Brief History of the Isle of Man

A 'steyned cloth' painted hanging in the Lord's Private Dining Room, Castle Rushen. Such hangings could be quickly prepared and hung and would have been used for the infrequent visits of the king of Mann. This reproduction shows the Stanleys' importance at the Battle of Bosworth. The Stanley horsemen are bottom left; one horseman in blue is carrying the eagle and child banner of the Stanleys

the Stanleys to Henry. It was partly to reward them for their help that Henry VII granted the Stanleys their earldom. That and the fact that the 1st Earl of Derby, as the fourth husband of Henry's mother, was the king's stepfather.

Those who have turned their coats once, may be suspected of doing so again and the Sir William Stanley who rode to Henry's help at Bosworth was later executed for suspected involvement with the pretender Perkin Warbeck. Thomas Stanley was understandably unhappy about Henry executing his brother and the growing suspicion between the two men led to an estrangement between Henry's mother, Lady Margaret, and her husband. Thomas Stanley's son by his first wife predeceased him so, when he himself died in 1504, the earldom passed to his twenty-year-old grandson, also Thomas.

The Tudor victor of the English Wars of the Roses, Henry had for years been ridding himself of any possible Yorkist claimant to the throne. By 1504, the English King had also placed the guilds and trade companies under crown supervision. Guilds were wealthy and, in the sixteenth century as today, wealth is often power. The 2nd Earl of Derby was the head of one of the most powerful families in England, with huge land holdings in Cheshire and Lancashire as well as being King of Mann. Henry VII had shown that not only was he on the look out for any challenge to his rule, he was not a man to be trifled with. Thomas Stanley's decision nominally to downgrade himself from king to lord might therefore have been a graceful gesture of submission while in reality relinquishing none of his privileges. In any case both titles still continued to be in use for some years.

Thomas Stanley first visited the Isle of Man in 1507 when he landed at Ronaldsway 'and ended a public tumult'. The fact of his visit seems to be generally accepted, but all the information we have comes from a traditional Manx ballad. The appropriate verse is:

Interior of Derby Fort on St Michael's Island. Originally one of Henry VIII's coastal fortifications it was refurbished and renamed during the English Civil War

> *'Ayns un thousane queig cheead as shiaght* (In fifteen hundred and seven)
> *She ayns mee ny Boaldiney ve* (And in the month of May)
> *Ghow eh thalloo ayns Roonsyssvie,* (He came on shore at Ronaldsway)
> *Er boirey'n theay hug eh slane fea.'* (And ended a public tumult)

As part of the rest of the ballad praises Stanley's person, wealth, display and military prowess it seems reasonable to conclude that the public tumult was ended by him to protect his Manx people rather than subjugate them. The bay where Stanley landed was named Derby-haven in his honour, and still is.

The Derby name was also attached to the circular mediaeval fort on St Michael's Isle built about 1540 to guard the entrance to Derbyhaven. The glacis or paved slope in front of Castle Rushen was built at around the same time. Both were created in response to English King Henry VIII's wish to build coastal defences around his domain which were capable of with-standing the growing threat posed by cannon fire. The original name of the fort does not appear to have survived, but it became known as Derby Fort after James, the 7th Earl, who refurbished it in 1644 at the time of the English Civil War.

Monastic memorial

As long as the church was able to defer to an authority outside the country, i.e. as long as it owed allegiance to the Bishop of Rome, the secular power's control over it was limited. All that changed in 1531 when Henry VIII was recognised as the Supreme Head of the Church in England. It is debatable whether Henry's supremacy in England legally affected the status of the church on Mann. On the other hand, the island's lord was one of Henry's subjects and it had already been established that tact was needed when dealing with the Tudors.

At first very little actually changed on Mann. Admittedly the church as a whole was no longer independent of the state and could not use the power of the pope to stymie the require-ments of the secular authorities. On the other hand, the island was conservative in the matter of religion, as was its lord. It was not until 1610, for example, that Manx clergy were permitted to marry; their English brethren had been allowed to do so since 1549. Edward Stanley, 3rd Earl of Derby and Lord of Mann at the time of the dissolution of the monasteries, was a staunch Catholic. By contrast the Bishop of Sodor and Man, Dr Thomas Stanley, could not be said to be a man of great spiritual worth. Bishop Stanley was probably Edward's illegitimate second cousin and appeared happy to go along with changes to religious practice as long as he was not penalised financially. The family presented him to several livings, probably in order to avoid paying for his keep themselves.

Once Henry VIII was head of the church, it was only a matter of time before he began casting covetous eyes at the wealth of the monasteries. Henry was hard up and wanted the monastic cash to finance his extravagant lifestyle. Like his father before him he was also eager to suppress any centres of power which might challenge his rule. In 1536 the First Suppression Act dissolving the lesser monasteries was passed by the English Parliament. The action had little or nothing to do with religion, but a great deal to do with power and money. A second Act was passed in 1539 dissolving those monasteries remaining.

On 9 April 1537, Abbot Robert of Furness 'with complete consent and assent conceded and surrendered the Monastery of Furness and all its inheritance in the Isle of Man' to Henry VIII. On 24 June 1540 the Abbot of Rushen Abbey and six monks were expelled from their monastic home. The abbot received a pension of ten pounds per year, the monks £1 6s 8d, a respectable sum for the time. The pensions were not only promised, they actually seem to have been paid, the money coming from the proceeds of the abbey land rentals. Interestingly the rents from the abbey lands continued to be collected but never seem

All that remains of the Chapter House, Rushen Abbey. The abbey buildings were cannibalised for building stone, so little remains above ground

to have been handed over to the English Crown, presumably disappearing into the coffers of the local bailiff, governor or possibly even the Lord of Man. This must have been one of the very few occasions when Henry didn't get what he wanted. The sea was a great protector.

The rent anomaly meant that Rushen abbey, was not only probably the last in the British Isles to be closed – Guisborough Priory in Cleveland seems to have been the last in England to close, on 8 April 1540 – but also the last to be formally dissolved. Rents from the abbeylands were still collected for the next seventy-one years until James I granted all the property to the

6th Earl of Derby in 1611. The continued collection of the rent indicates that the land was still worked, which was good news for the local labourers. In England, many of the monastic lay brethren and employees were thrown onto the streets as their homes were destroyed.

Once Rushen Abbey had been vacated, many of the monastic buildings were demolished and used as a source of building materials while its livestock and other moveables were also sold off. The silver from the abbey amounted to 'four chalices, one chrouche (the abbot's pastoral staff), one censer (also known as a thurible), one cross, two little headless crosses, one boat (a small box for holding incense), one hand and one bishop's head (both presumably reliquaries whose shape indicated the nature of the relic within), four cruets (for use during the mass to hold the wine and water), eleven spoons, two standing cups, two pocula with covers (drinking cups, possibly made of glass and chased with silver), one flat pece (a drinking vessel, particularly for wine), one salt, two masers (large wooden drinking cups or bowls with metal, probably silver, around the rim), one pix (to reserve and display the consecrated host)'. Edward Stanley purchased the lot for between £34 8s 5d to £37 8s 8d; reports vary about the exact amount. Perhaps the abbey silver ended up gracing the Earl's private chapel at the family seat of Knowsley Hall, Merseyside.

A hiccough in the Stanley succession

The 4th Earl of Derby was ten when the spoils of Rushen Abbey were being divided and sold. Eleven years later, in 1572, Henry Stanley inherited the Earldom and Lordship of Mann from his father and ruled quietly for the next twenty-one years. He did visit the island three times, in 1577, 1583 and 1585 to attend to various legal and financial matters, and was generally accounted a fair and even generous Lord. But unexciting.

His son, Ferdinando, 5th Earl of Derby ruled Mann for less than a year and his death in 1594 caused a problem in the Stanley succession. Incidentally, as a first name Ferdinando stands out like a neon sign among the more prosaic Thomases, Jameses and Johns normally given to the Stanley children. Elizabethans typically chose names which were common in their families and communities, apparently as a way of expressing connexion with those around them. Elizabethan children were normally named after a parent, godparent or close relative, for example, so the appearance of a Ferdinando is extraordinary. Why Henry and his wife Margaret chose such an unusual name for their son remains a mystery.

Ferdinando was only 35 when he died, and his sudden death was widely mooted to be due to poison administered in revenge for his refusal to support the Catholic cause. He left three daughters and a brother, but no son. The daughters and their uncle the 6th Earl all felt they had a right to Mann, so Elizabeth I, feudal overlord of the family, was left to adjudicate. During the deliberations a rival claim was raised by the Percy family, Earls of Northumberland. Back in 1405 Henry Percy, then King of Mann, had supported the rebellion against King Henry IV of England. The Stanleys had fought in support of Henry, helped suppress the rebellion, and gained Mann as a result (see chapter 4). The Northumberland family now argued that their ancestor had not been deprived of his titles until convicted of treason in absentia in 1406 and attainted. As a result, King Henry IV could not legally have granted Mann to the Stanleys in 1405 as its ownership by the Percys had not yet been rescinded. They wanted the island back.

Such an argument might have had weight with anyone but a monarch. Queen Elizabeth I was notoriously touchy about the rights of kings and was never likely to bow to a clever argument which upset the status quo and overturned the decisions of an anointed king in favour of the descendents of a convicted traitor. The Privy Council pointed out that the Percys did appear to be right about the date of the attainder, tactfully decided that Mann belonged to the monarch and carefully overlooked the Stanleys' near two-hundred-year reign. Queen Elizabeth, however, was too astute at political manoeuvring to want to decide between two of the most powerful families in her kingdom and probably alienate one of them. She gave up her right and batted the contending claimants back to the Privy Council.

The Law Lords on the Privy Council decided that 'the grant being by letters patent under the Great Seal of England, such right would descend according to the Common Law of England to the heirs general, and not to the heirs male'. Translated this meant that Ferdinando's eldest daughter Anne, rather than his brother William, had the right to rule the Isle of Man. Anne was fourteen when her father died, twenty three when Queen Elizabeth I died in 1603 and twenty seven when the Privy Council granted her the right to the Lordship of Mann. The four-year delay after Elizabeth's death might have been due to the complication that, under the will of Henry VIII and the Third Act of Succession, Anne Stanley was heir presumptive to the English throne. In other words, as the great, great granddaughter of Mary Tudor, Henry's sister, and after the death of Elizabeth, Anne Stanley should have been queen. Not being granted the crown of England, Anne might have been given the crown of Mann as a consolation prize.

William, who had become the 6th Earl of Derby thirteen years previously, agreed to purchase the Lordship of Mann, together with its rights, from his niece. For some reason, however, he had to wait until 1609. Many historians state that William had to wait until his niece came of age, but this seems unlikely as, in 1609, she would have been twenty nine. The delay may have been due to Anne's marriage in 1607 to Grey Brydges, the 5th Baron Chandos. He might have had something to say about giving up the lucrative rights to Mann.

All this wrangling took some time and James VI and I (VI of Scotland and I of England) now occupied the English throne. The king appointed a couple of caretaker Lords of Mann, Henry Howard and Robert Cecil for one year each, until William Stanley 6th Earl of Derby took over the role in 1609. He was confirmed in office the following year by an English act of parliament which stated: 'The said William Earle of Derbie [Ferdinando's brother] hath paid dyvers somes of money for their clayme, right, and title to the said isle, castle, peele, and lordship of Mann...' and confirmed '...forasmuch as the said isle and lordship of Mann hath long continued in the name and bloud of the said Earle [of Derbie], and to the end the same may continewe still by your Highness princely favour and gracious allowance...' The rule of the Stanleys resumed.

The First Manx Book
William Stanley purchased the Lordship of Mann from his niece, but doesn't seem to have cared much for the island he went to such trouble to procure. The 6th Earl may have been the titular head but the island was largely under the aegis firstly of his wife and later of his son. Probably the most important single event in William's reign was the publication in 1610 of the first book to be written in Manx. Even that was largely finished during the interregnum.

John Phillips, Bishop of Sodor and Man, was from North Wales and so had something of a headstart when it came to understanding Gaelic. Although not from Mann he took the trouble to learn Manx in order to be able to preach to his flock in a language he could be sure they understood; the men might have had a smattering of other languages, but the women and children would not, and Phillips knew that. He not only wanted the Manx people to understand his words, but also to understand the words of the church. The Book of Common Prayer in English had been published first in 1549 and contained in one volume all the services most often used. It had gone through a couple of revisions, reflecting the Tudor swings from Protestant to Catholic and back again, before a compromise was accepted by all church factions in 1559.

Bishop Phillips wanted a similar prayer book in Manx. So he decided to translate the English one.

It is difficult to realise now just how big a job the Bishop had taken on. Up to the mid sixteenth century, with the exception of the odd place name, Manx was purely an oral language. It was the language of the country, everyone spoke it, but nothing was written down. The administration of the island, the Manx statute books, the Tynwald records, etc., all were recorded in French or English. Church records, which went back further, had traditionally been in Latin. Irish and Scots Gaelic had both been transcribed since about the eighth century, but there was nothing in Manx at all.

As written languages, the Gaelic of Ireland and Scotland already possessed accepted orthographies which were similar to each other. As the third member of the goidelic group of Celtic languages, Manx could have fitted into a similar pattern. Bishop Phillips either didn't know that or didn't care to use it. Phillips therefore not only had to translate the English words and phrases into Manx equivalents, but had to invent phonetic and consistent spellings for the Manx words, using the English alphabet. It's as if French had never been written down and the French phrase *tête-à-tête* was today transcribed as *teta tet*, with the latter becoming the accepted spelling in certain regions. Phillips' efforts resulted in Manx today appearing very different from other Gaelic languages although in sound, structure and vocabulary Irish and Scots in particular are actually quite similar.

Church of St Adamnan, better known as Lonan Old Church. Adamnan was a seventh century Irish saint noted for celebrating Mass in Gaelic and translating religious works into the vernacular. Nine centuries later Bishop Phillips wanted to do something similar

Phillips was helped in his translation work by the Vicar of Kirk Michael, the Rev Hugh Cannell, who was not only a Manxman and clergyman, but who was also the bishop's nearest clerical neighbour. At this time Kirk Michael had no vicarage, but it's probably safe to assume that Cannell did not live too far away from his church and it was the nearest one to the bishop's residence of Bishopscourt. Translation was not made easier by the fact that there were two dialectic versions of Manx depending on whether speakers lived north or south of the island's spine of hills. The translation was completed in 1610, but does not appear to have been printed at the time. The fact that it wasn't printed doesn't necessarily mean that it wasn't used, however. In the early seventeenth century it was still very common practice for those wanting a copy of something, particularly something relatively short, to copy it out longhand.

It was one thing to write down a translation of the Book of Common Prayer but quite another to get others to read it. If Manx had been a purely oral language before, then its transcription

A Brief History of the Isle of Man

doesn't suddenly make Manx speakers literate in Manx even if they are so in English – and many wouldn't be. Bishop Phillip's letter to Robert Cecil, acting Lord of Man, says: 'The two Viccars Generall (Sr Wm Norres and Sr Wm Crowe) were asked by the Lieutennante whether they saw or knew of the Book of Common Prayer said to have been translated into the Manshe speech, they answered that they have seen the Book translated by the new Bishop of Sodor into Mannish. And Sr Wm Norres for his part further answereth that he could not read the same Book perfectly but here and there a word. And Sr Wm Crose for his part answereth that having the same Book a day or two before he could upon deliberate perusall thereof read some part upon it, and doth verily think that few else of the clergy can read that same Book for that it is spelled with vowels wherewith none of them are acquainted.' It was left to Rev. Cannell to teach Manx speakers to read their own language.

Modern tapestry in Holy Trinity Church, Patrick showing the Lord's Prayer in Manx

Although a later, and many would say greater, bishop, Bishop Wilson (see chapter 6) altered some of the Manx orthography so that the Manx of today appears slightly different, modern Manx versions of the Book of Common Prayer are still recognisably similar to that first book in Manx written by Phillips and Cannell. At the end of the nineteenth century, historian A.W. Moore provided an excellent comparative example in his *Historical Sketch of the Manx Language*:

Aer run ta ayns neau, kasserick gy row t'æn Ym. (Phillips' version)
Ayr am, t'ayns niau; Casherick dy row dt'Ennym. (1887 version)
Our Father which art in Heaven, hallowed be thy name. (English equivalent)

The Great Stanley

James Stanley represented his father in Manx affairs for fifteen years before he became the7th Earl and officially Lord of Mann in 1642. During his custodianship, to encourage the breeding of native horses, he instituted the first regular horse race in the world. 'The Derby' founded in 1780 by the 12th Earl might be famous as a race for three-year-olds at Epsom, but its precursor was the Manx Derby, founded in 1627 by the 7th Earl. The Manx Derby was held on what is now the Castletown Golf and Country Club on Langness. The seventh hole on the golfcourse is called the Racecourse as it is thought to mark the location of the original Derby racetrack.

James Stanley visited the Isle of Man far more than any other member of his family and lived there for some years. His reign was by no means a peaceful one; he clashed with the Manx-born governor of the island whom he himself appointed, and caused open resistance among the tenant farmers by interfering with the customs of how land was held and transferred. Nevertheless he was generally considered a just man, interested in the welfare of the Manx, and desirous to defend their island (and his own status) from the parliamentary rebels across the

water. On the Isle of Man he came to be known in Manx as *Y Stanlagh Moare*, The Great Stanley.

The disinterest of his father in the island, plus his mother's failing health and subsequent death, meant that James really began ruling Mann in 1627. Matters were largely peaceful at first. James visited the island periodically – a thing many of the Stanleys had not bothered to do – and had appointed Edward Christian, experienced sea

7th hole on the Castletown Golf and Country Club. It is called the Racecourse as it marks the course of the first Derby

captain and member of a large and influential Manx family, as lieutenant governor.

For five years the two men rubbed along well until Captain James of HMS *Lion's Whelp* accused Christian of dealing with pirates. Christian refuted the allegation and claimed that the alleged pirate had a properly signed letter of marque. A letter of marque was a government warrant which authorised the captain of a ship to seize the vessels of a hostile nation, and was considered just short of a declaration of war. Such a letter effectively nationalised piracy. It transformed evil pirates out for their own gain into patriotic privateers who divided their booty with the government, in return for legal protection. The difference is slight but important, and Christian would have been well aware of it; he'd been a privateer in his younger days.

The charge was serious enough for Christian to be summoned to appear at Whitehall on 14 February 1634 to answer it. He was too ill to go, a circumstance verified by a messenger despatched by James Stanley for the purpose. His illness may have been a convenience as the Manxman would anyway have probably not been too harsh on seafarers who dodged the laws of England.

Smuggling, rife in England since the imposition of a tax on wool exports in 1275 (and carried on since Saxon times), was simply unknown on Mann. Tynwald set the island's own tariffs and decided that it was legal to import any commodity which could be resold. Consequently there was no need to smuggle anything into the island. Because of the difference in the tax laws, smuggling into England and Scotland was honest trade on Mann and virtually every Manx family had some involvement with it (see also chapter 6). Smuggling is the illegal acquisition of goods by importation, while piracy is the illegal acquisition of goods by seizure. It's doubtful whether a good Manxman such as Christian would really consider them very different.

Events such as the accusation of 'trucking with a pirate' might have made Stanley a little wary of his lieutenant governor, but matters really came to a head in 1642 when Edward Christian was instrumental in stirring up the Manx to resist paying tithes. Tithes had long been a bone of contention (see chapter 4), largely because most of the funds raised went to senior churchmen such as the bishop, and ended up off island. Civil War had just broken out across the water, Stanley was in England raising men, arms and money for Charles I, and Christian

A Brief History of the Isle of Man

had been training the Manx militia at The Lhen in order to defend the island if necessary. Consequently his association with a riot in Douglas was a serious threat to national order in a time of war.

Christian had been replaced as lieutenant governor in 1639 by Radcliffe Gerard, but neither Gerard, nor the governor John Greenhalghe, had the power to redress the people's grievances. Stanley succeeded to the earldom in September 1642 and was in England through most of the winter fighting in the royalist cause around Manchester and in Lancashire and Cheshire. In June 1643 rumours reached King Charles that the Isle of Man might be invaded by the Scots and Stanley was ordered to fortify his realm for the king in exile. The Earl arrested Christian, who had been accused of using his influence over the militia to stir up revolt. Rather than bringing him before a jury for trial, Stanley had Christian tried by the Keys, at least one of which, Ewan Christian, was a family connexion. Even so The Twenty Four found Christian guilty, fined him one thousand marks and imprisoned him until the Lord of Man thought he should be released. It wasn't the last the island was to hear of him.

Bearing in mind the bloodshed going on across the water, the moderation of the Manx verdict is surprising. Stanley undoubtedly manoeuvred to retain absolute authority on the island, but did not suppress the disturbances with the vigour and violence which would have been normal for the time. He may have been pragmatic as well as humane. As Lord of Mann he may genuinely have been concerned for the welfare of his 'subjects', but may also have known that he could not afford the island to be disaffected and rebellious while civil war was raging in England. If the royalist cause failed, the Stanley family needed a bolthole.

Mann had been a traditional stepping stone for forces invading England from the west, and Oliver Cromwell knew as well as anyone that armies could be moved with less effort and far more quickly by water than on land. Stanley and the royalists wanted to make sure that the strategically-important island remained in their hands. The Earl recruited troops from among the Manx, and, in May 1644, Tynwald itself was called on to consider the best way to resist

Epsom racecourse, current home of the Derby

an invasion. Troops of cavalry and infantry were increased in size and seven camps were formed, one each at Knock y Doonee, Ramsey, Hanmerffould (which is probably somewhere between Sartfield and The Cronk), Knockaloe, Howstrake, Kirk Santan and Kirk Arbory (probably on a hill near Ballabeg). Two camps each week, one on each side of the island, were manned in rotation by the militia of each parish. In addition the old watch and ward lookout posts continued to be manned, several forts were built largely to protect harbours, and the 7th Earl even had a rudimentary navy.

During the seventeenth century, muskets and cannon finally ousted bows and armour from the battlefield. Mediaeval fortresses with their high walls were of little use as a defence against cannon; they presented too large a target without providing suitable platforms from which to fire back. Civil War forts were generally squat with thick walls which were protected from infantry attack by projecting gun emplacements or bastions. They tended to have a solid base made of earth or occasionally stone, and may also have had a wooden palisade around the top. The most famous and most complete remaining civil war fortification on Mann is also the least typical. Derby Fort on St Michael's Island was refortified from one of Henry VIII's coastal defences (see above). Other fortifications were built at Douglas (at the eastern end of what is now Fort Street, near the Victoria Pier), Ramsey and Point of Ayre and one inland at Ballachurry. Now called Kerroogarroo Fort (*kerroo garroo* means 'rough quarter' in Manx), the fort at Ballachurry, is a model civil war fortification and, although best viewed from the air, clearly shows the geometric shape of the type of fort known as a sconce. The site for Kerroogarroo Fort was chosen as the best place from which to defend the northern end of the island. Loyal to exiled Charles II, who had inherited the English crown on the execution of his father, Stanley intended to hold the Isle of Man for the royalists come what may.

He failed of course, but only because the royalist cause failed. James Stanley moved his wife and children to Mann and joined them there in July 1644, after the Battle of Marston Moor. The royalists lost the battle and with it their hold on the north of England. In 1649, the English parliament demanded that Mann be surrendered to them. Stanley refused, instead maintaining his loyalty to Charles II and offer-

Kerroogarroo Fort, formerly called Ballachurry Fort. A rough square with arrow-shaped earthworks pointing outward from each corner, only from the air is its defensive shape clearly visible

ing a haven to all royalists who wished it. From 1644 until 1651 Stanley and his Countess lived in Castle Rushen maintaining the cavalier way of life in defiance of the puritan parliament across the water and, incidentally, causing bad feeling among his Manx subjects who were responsible for provisioning the castle.

In 1651 Charles Stuart made an ill-advised attempt to regain his father's throne by invading England from Scotland. Few royalists responded to his call, but the Lord of Mann was one of them. He and some of his Manx troops sailed to England in April, joined battle at Wigan in August and Worcester in September, and was defeated both times. After Worcester, Stanley was captured and held in Chester Castle before being tried by court martial. The charge was one of high treason against the Commonwealth of England as, despite an Act prohibiting correspondence with Charles Stuart, the Earl had continued to contact royalists abroad. Found guilty James Stanley was ordered to be 'put to death by severing his head from his body at the market place in the town of Boulton in Lancashire upon Wednesday the 15th of this instant October, about the hour of one o'clock of the same day.' Sentence was carried out despite appeals for clemency and despite his claim that he only surrendered on promise of quarter. The Great Stanley is buried in Ormskirk parish church, his body in a coffin and his head in a separate casket.

The Manx right to their own land

The Great Stanley might have been acknowledged as a man of honour and loyalty, and mindful of the welfare of his people, but his dismissal of ancient Manx customs concerning land tenure and transfer stirred up so much trouble that only his death saved him from having to deal with out-and-out revolt. The Lord of Mann had an odd contradictory relationship with the Manx people; Stanley as a person was generally liked, Stanley as a landlord was cordially detested.

The laws surrounding land tenure on Mann differed from those in the rest of Britain and were very complex. Simply put they amounted to the fact that no-one apart from the land barons, i.e. the church and the Lord of Mann, actually owned any Manx land. The ordinary people were tenants, holding their land by custom on three kinds of payment. Firstly they had to provide food for the island's garrisons and the Lord's retinue, secondly they had to spend a certain number of days working on repairing public infrastructure such as on the castles, roads, harbours, etc., and thirdly they had to pay a fixed rent in cash, kind and/or service.

Surrounded by water the island's farming population tended to be more static than that in the rest of Britain. A move to the island was a major upheaval for country people, a break with family and familiar surroundings which contrasted with the gradual drift of a populace in

View from Castle Rushen up the Silverburn. Used as a royalist stronghold during the English Civil War the castle provided sanctuary to many royalists ousted from their own country

larger countries who intermarry, move from nearby villages and fill vacuums in neighbouring societies. Mann's farming population tended to be limited to those born there. Emigration was common, immigration far less so as non-Manxmen were not allowed the same status and privileges as natives. Farmers and land workers were therefore in a stronger negotiating position than their peers across the water as there were fewer potential tenants for farms. Consequently landowners had tended to allow their tenants more leeway, such as being able to pass their land to sons and grandsons, for example.

Gradually, therefore, tenants who had been working the same farm for generations came to consider the land as their own and, more seriously from the Lord's point of view, began treating it as such by selling or exchanging parcels of it. One custom which had grown up was the 'tenure of the straw'. By it a tenant parting with land delivered a straw grown on it to the manorial court to indicate that he had relinquished it, and the new tenant had the right to take charge of it.

Various laws had been passed to try and regulate the land question, but little had made much difference until the 7th Earl decided to sort things out. Naturally, considering himself as the official landowner, he wanted things to be sorted out in his favour. He put together what would now be called a marketing campaign, emphasising that under the straw tenure the Lord had the right to evict families immediately, but with a lease, tenure was more secure. He also amended rents for certain terms of years to persuade tenants to change to leaseholders. Many did so, erroneously believing that they would be making their families more secure. In fact, by adopting the leases rather than continuing with the straw tenure they gave up their customary right of inheritance.

Matters were exacerbated by the influx of additional troops and any cavaliers looking for sanctuary. Under their laws of tenure, the Manx people had to feed those housed in Castle Rushen and the effort of providing provisions for so many extra mouths for protected periods was considerable. News of the successful rebellion across the water must have encouraged the idea of a Manx rebellion to those struggling under increasing demands for provisions, foreign fortification, and legalised theft of their livelihoods. The execution of Charles I, Stanley's overlord, was the result of rebellion against royal rule. Stanley's own execution was the one event which could have prevented him from facing a rebellion against his own.

CHAPTER 6

THE STANLEYS RISE AGAIN

The Commonwealth had placed the Isle of Man under the command of Thomas Fairfax in 1649, two years before the execution of the 7th Earl, but little had been done about imposing Commonwealth rule. Stanley's eldest son Charles was around twenty three when his father died, and was living with many of the exiled English court in France, so in practice his mother, the dowager Countess of Derby, ruled the island. She had already successfully defended a siege on Lathom House, the family's Lancastrian seat, and probably felt that she was quite as capable of organising the defence of the Isle of Man.

What the countess did not expect was a rebellion in her own backyard – almost literally. The official residence of the Stanley family was Castle Rushen, but across the bay in Ronaldsway was the farm of William Christian, known to his family as Illiam Dhone, or Brown William. William was the son of the Deemster Ewan Christian of Milntown, who was one of those who tried Edward Christian (see chapter 5). Like many Manxmen Illiam Dhone was taken in by The Great Stanley's marketing campaign and was persuaded to hold his farm on a lease for three lives rather than under the old custom of straw tenure. The earl appreciated William's easy adherence to what Stanley considered the right, and appointed him Receiver General and Collector for the island, effectively giving him the power to collect all land revenues and many port dues, plus customs duties. William must have performed his duties conscientiously as, when Stanley left the island in 1651, he placed William in charge of the militia. Hindsight is a wonderful thing, but after his experience with Edward, another member of the Christian family, it might have been thought that the Lord of Mann would have been less complacent of his own authority.

Illiam Dhone, Kirk Malew

Once news of The Great Stanley's capture reached Mann, order on the island broke down. The main problem was that, for all they had been co-existing for many years, the Stanley family and the Manx people did not trust each other. Without informing the Deemsters, Tynwald or any senior Manxmen, Charlotte the dowager Countess, offered to surrender the Isle of Man to Colonel Duckenfield, the representative of the English Parliament, in return for her husband's life. William and his Manx colleagues suspected the countess's actions and were worried that the island would be surrendered and the Manx people stripped of their ancient liberties. The Countess disregarded natural Manx concerns over their homeland, seeing its governance as merely an extension of Stanley power, while Illiam Dhone and his colleagues stirred up insurrection.

The Manx acted quickly and soon held most of the Civil War forts built to defend the island and manned largely by islanders. They recognised, however, that the storming of the substantial castles of Rushen and Peel, garrisoned as they were by imported troops, was beyond them.

Ramsey Bay. English parliamentarians landed here before besieging Peel Castle and Castle Rushen

Like the countess, they also contacted Colonel Duckenfield. He'd been sent to the island with troops to take it by force if necessary, and was already anchored in Ramsey Bay. Perhaps the Manx leaders' respect for the Manx parliament of Tynwald made them believe that they would get a better deal from English parliamentarians than from the relict of a minor king. Whatever the reason Illiam Dhone notified Duckenfield that English parliamentarian troops would be allowed to land unopposed, providing that he would guarantee the laws and liberties of the Manx as existed before James Stanley tried to impose leasehold tenancy on them.

Duckenfield agreed to the terms – who wouldn't? – landed his troops with some difficulty in stormy weather and immediately besieged both Peel and Rushen castles. Tradition states that the parliamentary forces stabled their horses at the Raggatt, Peel, but it was Castle Rushen which was the stronger fortification and in which Charlotte Stanley was still defiant. On 29 October 1651, one day after the siege began, the Colonel wrote to the Countess inviting her to surrender Castle Rushen and, formally, the island. It was unfortunate that his letter contained the words 'the late Earl of Derby', as this was the first Charlotte knew of her husband's death. Grief stricken she at first refused to surrender but when she learned that the castle garrison was reluctant to fight, ceded victory on condition that she, together with her children, friends and servants, had 'liberty to transport themselves for England, there to make what application to the Parliament she shall think fit, and from thence to passe into Holland, or France, if she please'. The fall of Castle Rushen on 3 November 1651 gave Charlotte Stanley, Dowager Countess of Derby, the distinction of being the last person to surrender to parliamentary forces during the English Civil War.

The English Parliament had already granted the Isle of Man to Thomas Fairfax, but also confirmed what Duckenfield had promised Illiam Dhone, namely that the Manx would retain their laws providing they be 'equitable and just'. William Christian (Illiam Dhone) retained his office as receiver and, between 1656 and 1658, was also the island's governor. Deemsters John and William Christian (not Illiam Dhone) were summoned to London to represent Mann before the English Parliament, while Edward Christian was released from his eight-year incarceration in Peel Castle. If November 1651 was a terrible month for the Stanleys, it was an excellent one for the Christian family.

The Isle of Man was cushioned from the most extreme puritanism of the English Parliament by distance and tardiness. The Commonwealth had already been in existence for two years before Fairfax assumed control of the island and parliamentarians, dealing with war with the Dutch, the continued agitation of Charles II who had been crowned in Scotland, and the question of a successor to Oliver Cromwell, had little time for a small island on the fringes of their new domain.

The Stanleys rise again

The 7th Earl's support for the royalist cause might have cost him his head, but it saved his inheritance for his heirs. When Charles II resumed the English throne on 29 May 1660, those who had supported him in adversity were suitably rewarded. James Stanley had been executed in the royalist cause, but his son Charles was confirmed as 8th Earl and all his titles and estates, including the Lordship of Man, returned to him.

Two topics immediately became prominent: how to handle the question of land tenure, and what to do about Illiam Dhone. The former was a problem which would dog Manx rulers for the next forty years, as the Lord of Mann tried to insist on his right to find and change tenants at will, while the Manx maintained their right of inheritance. The latter, however, was a question of rebellion against not only the ruler of the island at the time, but also his own mother. The new earl could and did deal with it, to his own if not to the island's satisfaction.

Hango Hill. William Christian (Illiam Dhone) was executed here in 1663. The ruins postdate the execution

William Christian (Illiam Dhone) had been off island for a number of years, but was arrested in September 1662, when he returned to his homeland. On 29 August 1660, in an effort to heal factional rifts and prevent further violence, An Act of Free and General Pardon, Indemnity and Oblivion was passed by the English Parliament stating: 'that noe Crime whatsoever committed against His Majesty or His Royall Father [i.e. Charles II or I] shall hereafter rise in Judgement or be brought in Question against any of them.' Christian had been assured that the Act of Indemnity would protect him against prosecution for his leadership of the Manx Rebellion of 1651. Unfortunately the act mentioned only crimes against the kings of England. The Lordship of Mann was not mentioned and the Stanley who held it was legally able to arrest William Christian. He was imprisoned in Castle Rushen and brought to trial on 26 November 1662.

Probably aware that his brother and nephew, Deemster John Christian and his son Edward, had already sailed for England to appeal to the king for clemency, William refused to enter a plea at his trail. He may possibly have been trying to delay matters until the result of the petition was known, but if so appears again to have been badly advised. The Keys declared that, in the circumstances of an accused person refusing to plead, his life and goods were at the mercy of the Lord of Mann. The remaining Deemster, Norris, was instructed to pronounce sentence. For treason – which is what Christian's crime effectively was – the sentence could only be death. William Christian, aka Illiam Dhone, was duly sentenced to be hung, drawn and quartered. On 2 January 1663 at Hango Hill he was executed, the sentence commuted to death by firing squad to spare his wife distress. Instruction from Charles II that the Act of Indemnity did indeed also apply to the Isle of Man and its Lord arrived too late to save Christian. The ruling did however secure the Christian property, forfeited under attainder, to his sons.

Religious belief – and practice

Eager not to appear to benefit personally from the death of Illiam Dhone, Charles Stanley passed Christian's confiscated property to the Bishopric of Sodor and Man. At this time the Bishop was either Samuel Rutter, who had been chaplain to the late earl and afterwards to the dowager countess, or his successor Isaac Barrow, uncle of the famous theologian of the same name and with whom he is often confused. The exact date of Bishop Rutter's death is not known but was 1662 or 1663. Presumably whoever the bishop was, he had to give the land back!

After Bishop Parr's death in 1643, Bishopscourt had been used as the summer residence of the Lord of Mann. The next eighteen years saw England controlled by the Commonwealth. Bishops were not recognised by the puritan church, so Bishopscourt was used by the officers sent by the English Parliament to govern the island. On the Restoration, when bishops were once again being consecrated, Bishopscourt again became the official residence of the Bishop of Sodor and Man.

Bishop Rutter's tomb in St German's cathedral, Peel Castle. He wrote his own Latin inscription which, translated, says: 'In this house which I have borrowed from my brothers the worms/ in the hope of the resurrection to life/ lie I SAM by divine grace Bishop of this Island./Stay reader, behold and laugh at the Bishop's palace.'

A Brief History of the Isle of Man

While not far from Peel and its harbour, Bishopscourt was not very handy for Douglas, particularly in an age with few roads and virtually no wheeled transport. It was impossible for the resident bishop to know accurately which boats were leaving from Douglas harbour and when they sailed. In ecclesiastical records dated 1405, the owner of Kirby, near Old Kirk Braddan, is mentioned as bound to offer hospitality to the Lord Bishop whenever he travelled to and from the island via Douglas. Bad weather could mean such hospitality extending for several days or even weeks. The regulation persisted for the next four hundred years, only being commuted to a small annual fee at the end of the nineteenth century.

The Manx church did not suffer the iconoclasm of the English churches where images were torn down and destroyed, but likewise did not experience the extreme laxity signalled by the Restoration of the monarchy and the relief from rigid Puritanism experienced in 1660. The biggest effect of Puritanism on the island was the influx of Quakerism. George Fox founded the Society of Friends in 1648 – incidentally the term 'Quakers' comes from a sermon given by Fox in 1650 when he told his followers to 'tremble at the word of the Lord'. Although no-one of any religion on the Isle of Man was martyred for their faith, the Quakers were very much persecuted. Most Manx Quakers lived in the parish of Maughold, and their burial ground, *Ruillic ny Quakeryn*, was donated by William Callow who is himself buried there. Only one headstone is visible and that was erected long after the event, but its inscription encapsulates the experience

Quaker burial ground, up the hill from Ballajora

of the Manx Quakers. It says: 'William Callow of Ballafayle 1629-1676 suffered long persecution, frequent imprisonment and finally banishment from his native island for his faith.'

The persecution started under Fairfax in 1658 when the governor, the celebrated Manx patriot and freedom fighter Illiam Dhone, prohibited Quakers from meeting, and anyone else from receiving Quakers into their houses. Quakers were also fined and imprisoned for refusing to attend church. Persecution continued under Charles Stanley who seems particularly to have disliked the Quakers, possibly fearing more civil unrest on Mann. In a letter replying to one from Prince Rupert, the earl says that he 'would not have that place [i.e. the Isle of Man] endangered to be infected with Schism and Heresy, which it might be liable to if Quakers should be permitted to reside there.' One of the elders of the Friends, the William Callow of the headstone in the Quaker burial ground, appealed to the Duke of York (afterwards James II) and Prince Rupert. Despite the intervention of Duke and Prince on the Quakers' behalf, Stanley refused Callow's appeal and in 1665 the Quakers were transported, very much against their will, to Dublin or Whitehaven.

Callow may have been forced off the island, but he did return. On 15 March 1672 Charles II issued his Royal Declaration of Indulgence in an attempt to extend religious liberty to non-conformists. Callow and the Quakers, hoping to take advantage of it, returned to Mann. The king was forced by parliament to withdraw the Declaration the following year but by then the Manx Quakers had determined to stay. Relief from persecution finally came in 1688 by the passing of 'An Act for Exempting their Majesties Protestant Subjects, Dissenting from the Church of England, from the Penalties of certain laws.' It is better known as the Toleration Act.

Leaders in learning

Before the seventeenth century, education was in the hands of the clergy who were paid to teach the sons of those of the well-to-do who thought education worth bothering about; clerics might also offer free tuition to bright boys from poorer families. Girls were educated at home. One of the earliest schools recorded on the island is mentioned in the will of Philip Christian, a Manxman working in London as a clothworker. In his will, dated 1655, he stated: 'If it shall happen that there be not a Free School maintained for the teaching of children in the Towne of Peele, then my will is that the twenty pounds a year…be paid by the said Company of Cloth-workers towards the maintenance of the said schools.' The wording seems to indicate that Peel had one of the few schools existing to educate children from non-wealthy families, but that the fees were still out of the reach of poor families. Christian wanted education in his home town to be available for all. Unusually he included girls in his educational wishes, as he also gave one pound per year for five years 'for buying of small books, pen, ink and paper, or what shall be thought most fit by the minister and school-emaster of the town of Peele… for the use of the poorest men's sons and daughters…'

Clothworkers Hall, London. Philip Christian would have been familiar with the area although not with this building; it is the sixth on the site. Christian may even have met one of the guild's young members, Samuel Pepys

Christian was not alone in wishing to im-prove the education of his countrymen; the Bish-op of Sodor and Man agreed with him. Bishop Isaac Barrow, appointed in 1663, was appalled at the low standard of education in the island gener-ally and among the clergy in particular. Bishop William Russell, three centuries earlier, would have sympathised, as he had similar problems and had to accept less well-educated men in or-der to be able to appoint priests who could speak Manx (see chapter 4). In England the quality of the clergy was highly variable, largely because livings were often purchased and it was not unusual for a young man to be promised a living before he was ordained or even while still a child, regardless of his fitness for the post.

Bishop Barrow determined to improve matters and established a number of schools, in-cluding a free school at Castletown. Much of the money needed to fund the schools was raised from benefactors – Charles II of England gave £100, Charles Stanley, Lord of Mann made over certain tithes and, according to Bishop Wilson a successor to the see about twenty-five years after Barrow, 'he collected amongst the English nobility and gentry six hundred pounds, the interest of which maintains an academic master'. Not content with that, in 1672 the bishop – Barrow had been succeeded by Henry Bridgman in 1671 – induced Stanley to insist that his tenants send their children to school or face a fine, effectively making education compulsory.

A Brief History of the Isle of Man

Interior of the Old Grammar School, Castletown. Originally the town church for the settlement which grew up around Castle Rushen it had been used as a school since at least 1570

Children in England and Wales had to wait until 1870, Irish children until 1892, for compulsory education. Compulsory education was introduced in Scotland in 1872, but Scottish education provision had for years been better than that south of the border.

Bishop Barrow also saw the need for additional support for boys training for the ministry. He used his own funds to purchase the farms of Ballagilley and Hango Hill, with the intention of using the profit from the estates to support and maintain such boys. The Deed drawn up in 1668 explains that he had given 'the profits of Ballagilly and Hango Hill…towards the maintenance and education of two Scholars at the University or Colledge of Dublin' and that, at the end of their training, they should 'returne if required by the Bishop or Trustees to serve their country or… to make full satisfaction for so much money as by them recd out of this guift during the said five years.' Not only was he improving the quality of his clergy, Bishop Barrow was also thereby ensuring, what many of those ruling the island had not, that profits made on and from Mann should benefit Mann.

The first Manx coins

Bishop Barrow in the Deed setting up his Trust, refers to money. He was writing in the year the Isle of Man first produced its own coinage – not that this made the island unusual. Money as coin had been known since antiquity, but had moved in and out of use according to what else was going on at the time. Gold coins, regardless of their country of origin and irrespective of their face value, were usually acceptable anywhere purely for their value in precious metal. Public banks, i.e. ones underwritten by the government rather than firms set up by an individual, family or group of businessmen, had only been set up to regulate the production of coinage since around the beginning of the seventeenth century.

Low value coinage, the sort used by ordinary people, was less common and less negotiable beyond national or sometimes even local boundaries. In Ireland, for example, almost every town produced its own local penny and two-penny tokens, acceptable for goods locally, but derided elsewhere. Such tokens were current in Mann until 1668 when John Murrey, a Douglas merchant, issued his own pennies, which he stated to be equivalent in value to their English counterparts. The 'Murrey's pence' were made legal tender in 1679 by the Court of Tynwald which also outlawed private tokens.

The Old Mint, Langness. Manx coins were thought to have once been minted here. Presumably its remoteness made it easier to defend from putative plunderers

Coins were still in short supply however, as they left the island with traders when they were exchanged for purchased imported goods. At this time coins everywhere contained, or were supposed to contain, the worth in metal which the coin stated as its value; the transition from a coin being a unit of weight to it being a unit of value had not yet taken place. Because of the difficulty in maintaining a supply of good coins on Mann, the coinage was debased slightly and consequently, in the 1690s, devalued. English Imperial coinage divided each shilling into twelve pennies. Tynwald decreed that fourteen Manx pennies were required for each English shilling. Such remained the case until 1839.

Murrey's pence remained the island's official currency for thirty years. Then, in 1708, the Isle of Man government approached the Royal Mint, housed at that time in the Tower of London, and asked that coinage be issued for the Isle of Man. The Master of the Mint Sir Isaac Newton refused, possibly because he had his hands full overseeing the silver re-coinage of both England and Scotland at the time. Not to be dissuaded the Manx government went ahead on its own and in 1709 issued £200 worth of halfpennies (112,000 halfpennies) and £300 worth of pennies (84,000 pennies). As it was not official coinage issued by the Royal Mint it did not have Queen Anne's head on the obverse. Neither did it have the head of the 10th Earl of Derby, the Lord of Mann. Instead the coins were issued with the Stanley crest of the eagle and child on one side and the three legs of Mann on the other.

A snapshot of Manx life

In the seventeenth century houses for ordinary Manx people were small, single storey dwellings, often only two rooms with a beaten earth floor and a low loft in the roof space above. They were built of local stone and thatched with locally-produced straw, often wheat straw. High winds on the island led to the tradition of leaving stones jutting out just beneath the roof line to which the twisted straw ropes used for securing the thatch could be anchored. Many of the traditional cottages still surviving in Cregneash, for example, were built at around the time the first government-issue Manx coinage was being produced.

There was not a huge Manx middle class, but several Manx families had grown to prominence, and a number of incomers had been appointed either for their specialist knowledge or because they were favoured by the Stanley family. An inventory taken of the Rectory, Andreas in 1677 provides an interesting glimpse of what might be called middle-class Manx houses in the seventeenth century. William Urquhart, Archdeacon of Mann rebuilt the house in 1666 and was probably still living there eleven years later. The rectory had five rooms: the *Thie Mooar*, or Great Hall; the *Greinnagh* or Solar, a room set apart for the ladies of the family and which

A Brief History of the Isle of Man

often provided the best light for fine needlework; the *Chamyr*, often spelt *Shamyr*, which was used as the master's study or office – the word 'chamber' has a similar root; the *Chamyr Seose* or master bedroom (*seose* means 'being up'; the sense here means 'upstairs') and the *Chamyr Beg* or small bedroom. The study had an oak table, a chest, a settle, two chairs with arms but probably not armchairs in the sense that they would not have been upholstered, and several stools. The two bedrooms had wooden bedsteads with feather mattresses, chests and stools. All four of the smaller rooms had curtains and rugs on the floor.

The Great Hall was flagged and covered each day with what were called fresh rushes but which were more likely to be marram grass, the old ones being removed and either burnt or composted. There was a large *chiollagh* or open hearth for a fire of peat and wood on which all the cooking was done. The Great Hall was the living room of the household, in which they also cooked and ate. It contained two long trestle tables, a small round table, two cupboards, a linen press, two chairs with arms, a settle, two chests and several stools. The women of the household also kept their spinning wheels for flax, hemp and wool in the Great Hall.

The rectory estate included a small farm with cattle, horses, sheep, poultry and bees to supply the household. The rector also kept a small fishing boat at the Lhen Beach. Clocks were scarce and the family relied on the sundial, ringing bells to inform those working outside of the times of meals and when they should start and stop work. Even as late as the mid eighteenth century there were virtually no wheeled vehicles on the Isle of Man. Bishop Wilson is credited with importing the first carriage, around 1749 when he was about 76. Even then he often travelled about the island by Manx pony.

Wages for ordinary Manx people were in general lower than for similar work in England. True the cost of living was greater in England, but not so much so that the Manx were not

The furthest building is Harry Kelly's cottage, Cregneash. A typical Manx dwelling and the first to be acquired by the Manx government to be opened as a museum

poorly paid. Even so the island population was generally healthy and, apart from during times of great hardship, appeared to have few beggars. Farming, fishing and mining were still the main occupations, with most of the population engaged in the first two. There were also a number of cottage industries including spinning and weaving, particularly of flax and linen.

The problem of land tenure, brought into prominence in 1630 by The Great Stanley while caretaking the island for his father (see chapter 5) had still not been resolved decades later. Not only was the land question bad for social harmony, it was bad for the land itself. With no guarantee that they or their children would be allowed to remain on the same property, farmers spent little on improving the land and did the minimum maintenance they could get away with. For a nation which relied heavily on farming, agricultural neglect was a disaster. The importance of good husbandry received promotion and emphasis from a rather unlikely source. In 1698 Thomas Wilson was appointed the Bishop of Sodor and Man. Even today, Bishop Wilson, with his combination of practical common sense, deep faith and active compassion, is considered the best bishop the island has ever had. He was also a very useful link between the Manx people and the ruling family. Bishop Wilson had been both the Stanley family chaplain and the current earl's tutor, and his genuine interest in solving the problems of the Manx people gained their trust.

The bishop was the son of a farmer and turned Bishopscourt farm into a model from which everyone could learn. James Stanley, the 10th Earl, was much more sympathetic to the land problem than his brother the 9th Earl had been and indicated as much to his old tutor Bishop Wilson. In 1703 a small deputation assembled consisting of Bishop Wilson, John Stevenson of Balladoole, Ewan Christian of Lewaigue House, and the latter's relative another Ewan Christian who had inherited property in Milntown and also owned Ewanrigg Hall in Cumberland. All held large tracts of Manx land, all were interested in keeping and improving it and all went to see Stanley in England. The result of their negotiations was the Act of Settlement, sometimes called the Manx Magna Carta. By it, many of the rights of land ownership were effectively transferred to the farmers who worked it. Such farmers could buy and sell land or pass it on to their children as they chose, without an overlord's interference. Only the Lord of Mann's right to certain fines was upheld, a payment which did not then carry any stigma of punishment, but which can be understood to be similar to taxation. Even today the 1703 Act of Settlement is considered a vitally important component in the legal ownership of Manx land.

The last of the Stanleys

James Stanley, 10th Earl of Derby was a soldier and politician and, like most of his family, more interested in various appointments in England than in visiting the island of which he held lordship. He succeeded to the title after the death of his brother William and was the last of the Stanley name to rule Mann.

1707 saw the Act of Union which united England and Scotland. It was also a century which involved much of Britain in costly foreign wars. The British government was desperately short of funds (nothing new there) and so decided to increase taxation to raise more money (also not new). One of the easiest taxes to levy was on goods purchased. The tax was divided into two categories, customs duties levied on imported goods, and an excise tax levied on domestic consumption. Purchasers therefore not only had to pay tax twice on some goods, but found that the tax was often more than half of the price they paid. Naturally people resented the extra cost and just as naturally tried to avoid paying it. Smuggling grew from a few fishermen bringing home the odd luxury for their family and neighbours into a large-scale, well organised and highly profitable business.

The Isle of Man in the middle of the Irish Sea was ideally positioned to take advantage of the high import duties imposed by the government in Westminster. Large trading vessels could and did land with impunity in the various Manx ports and along the island's coast. Having paid the much-lower duties on the island (or not) it was an easy matter to reorganise cargo into smaller vessels and slip across the sea to waiting customers in England and Scotland.

In a gesture of good faith, and in response to strong protests from across the water, Tynwald passed an act in 1711 prohibiting the shipment of foreign goods from Mann to Great Britain unless the correct duties were paid to the British government. The Act made little difference, as the Keys almost certainly could have predicted, and was probably intended only to show the smiling face of co-operation while still dealing under the counter. As the Act produced no concessions from the British government (which was possibly not taken in) to improve the legal trade of the Isle of Man, it was suspended in 1714.

Almost every Manx family had some seafaring connexion and virtually all seafarers were involved with some sort of trade, legal and otherwise. The Quayle family of Castletown, for example, built Bridge House in the early part of the 18th century as a result of the profits of smuggling (see chapter 7). Quayles also owned the estates of Crogga and Ballashamrock House both of which overlooked Port Soderick and were only a short distance from the shore. The Christian family had gone one better and purchased Ewanrigg Hall in Cumbria, just up the hill from the small hamlet of Ellenfoot, a major centre of smuggling and handy for boats landing from the Isle of Man. Ellenfoot is now better known as Maryport.

Balladoole House. Residence of John Stevenson, one of those negotiating the 1703 Act of Settlement. One of the oldest continuously-occupied estates on the island and in the ownership of the Stevenson family from 1334 to 1972. This is the back!

It was the smuggling activities of the Manx, and more particularly their success, which led to the end of the island's independence from direct rule by the English crown. James Stanley, like his brother, died without male issue – his only son had died of smallpox in 1710 – and so in 1736 the lordship of Mann descended to James Murray, a Scottish cousin and the 2nd Duke of Atholl. James was the third son, but his only surviving elder brother William was a prisoner in the Tower of London for taking part in the Jacobite rebellions in favour of the Old and Young Pretenders, James Stewart and his son Charles. A younger brother, George, was also fighting for the Jacobite cause. James Murray avoided attainder by being a supporter of King George II; he later fought under the Duke of Cumberland to help defeat the Jacobite army, and his own brothers, at the Battle of Culloden in April 1746.

Visits from the Lord of Mann had become increasingly rare, but the new Lord did come

Crogga House. Owned but never inhabited by the Quayle family the house overlooks Port Soderick. The original house was in the current garden and was used as a store for trade and contraband goods

to the island and was present at a meeting of Tynwald, despite some truly foul weather. In the twenty-eight years during which Murray was Lord of Mann the level of smuggling grew to epic proportions. The Lords of the Treasury of England tried to persuade him to sell the island back to the English crown but Murray refused. According to his heir he 'always declared that no temptation of gain could induce him to give up so ancient, so honourable, and so noble a birth-right such as no subject of the crown of England now has, or ever had'. As was the case of the last Stanley however, James Murray's sons predeceased him. When he died in 1764 his titles, including the lordship of Mann, passed to a nephew who was also his son-in-law.

Almost as soon as John Murray 3rd Duke of Atholl had inherited, he was contacted by the Lords of the Treasury about the sale of the island. Unlike his uncle, however, the English government had a lever they could use against the 3rd Duke. John's father, was the George Murray who had been part of the Jacobite army twenty years earlier and had been attainted for it. Desperate to stop the haemorrhaging of tax revenue caused by the Manx smugglers, the English government intimated that, unless John sell the island, his right of inheritance to it and possibly to his Scottish holding as well, could be re-examined in view of his father's attainder. As an additional persuasion the British parliament passed what became known on the island as the Mischief Act. By it revenue men were given the right to stop and search every boat arriving at or leaving Manx ports. Murray had little choice but bow to what was effectively a compulsory purchase order.

In 1765 the British parliament passed the Isle of Man Purchase Act, known as the Act of Revestment, reabsorbing the lordship of Mann into the English crown and compensating the Murrays to the tune of £70,000. A proposal had been made to annex the island to the

English county of Cumberland, but Sir George Moore, Speaker of the House of Keys, secured recognition of Manx independence to the relief of the islanders. Interestingly John Christian, grandson of the Ewan Christian of Milntown who helped negotiate the Manx Magna Carta (see above) was High Sheriff for Cumberland in 1766. Could such a politically influential man have been one of those suggesting the annex?

Under the Revestment Act the Duke of Atholl surrendered 'the Island, Castle, and Peel of Man, with all the Lordships thereto belonging, together with the royalties, regalities, franchises, liberties, and sea-ports appertaining to the same, and all other hereditaments and premises therein particularly described and mentioned as holden under the several grants thereof, or any other title whatsoever, reserving only their lands, inland waters, fisheries, mines, mills, minerals, and quarries according to their present right therein, felon goods, deodands, waifs, strays, and wrecks at sea, together with the patronage of the bishopric and of the other ecclesiastical benefices in the Island, to which they were entitled.'

For such privileges as he retained, Atholl had to pay £122 12s 2d per annum, plus the two coronation falcons (see chapters 5 and 8). The Revestment Act brought to an end over 350 years of family rule, although it did not end the Stanley/Atholl connexion with the island, which ceased only in 1828 (see chapter 7). For once the Manx people and their former ruler were in complete agreement. Both deeply resented the compulsory purchase of the island, although for very different reasons. Murray resented being cheated out of an inheritance before he'd even had time to enjoy it, while his former subjects were dismayed by the end of their lucrative trade. The Manxmen's free trade had cost them much of their independence. A jingle often repeated at the time was:

> 'The babes unborn will rue the day
> The Isle of Man was sold away.'

For the third time in its history, the Isle of Man was sold. Almost exactly five hundred years earlier, Alexander III had purchased the island with the intention of making a profit from it. History was set to repeat itself, as the Manx people were rightly wary of a new master whose sole interest in the island was the revenue to be made from it.

CHAPTER 7

THE ENGLISH, EMIGRATION AND ENTREPRENEURS

The Manx were right to be concerned about their island's change of ownership. Within a very few years customs men had recouped in revenue duty the money paid to the Atholls by the Revestment Act, and a lot more beside.

The administrative changes were far reaching and rapid. To begin with, executive power was removed from Tynwald, in fact if not at first explicitly. British administrators took over the organisation of the island. British rules were applied and the Westminster parliament began to make decisions which had previously been the prerogative of the Keys. For over eight hundred years the Keys had been influencing the laws of the island (see chapter 3). They had not always been successful or heeded, and had frequently been ignored, but had never before been completely discounted. When Mann was sold to the British crown, Tynwald was removed from the judicial process. Overnight Manxmen ceased to have any say in the governance of their own island. Small wonder they were annoyed.

Changes on the way

A flurry of acts followed the transference of ownership, most of them designed to raise taxes and make sure people paid them. In 1765 alone, acts were passed to check smuggling; discontinue the pecuniary advantages granted to those exporting corn to Mann; ensure the correct taxes were paid on the sales of wines, spirits and salt; secure and raise customs and excise revenue; and allow certain goods to be exported from Mann to the rest of Britain without the payment of duty. The wish to encourage the manufacture of linen on the island was particularly mentioned in the 'Act for the better securing and further improvement of the Revenues of Customs, Excise, Inland and Salt Duties; and for encouraging the Linen Manufactures of the Isle of Man…' Such encouragement was rare however and, in 1767, the Westminster parliament passed an act to levy new customs duties – other Acts had been to improve the collection of existing taxes – the first time non-Tynwald legislation had imposed taxes on the people of the island.

If the raft of new non-Manx legislation were not enough there must also have been an influx of new non-Manx administrators. Westminster would almost certainly not have trusted a Manx organisation to impose the new English laws and would have sent its own civil servants to ensure taxes were imposed and penalties paid. The new administrators would have been highly unlikely to speak the local language, and would probably have seen no reason to learn it. All administration would have been conducted in English and any Manxman who wanted to query or debate any decision, or gain a post in the new administration would have to be familiar with that tongue. A probably unforeseen consequence of the Revestment Act was the beginning of the demise of Manx Gaelic as a first language.

With the seat of power now 300 miles away and little communication faster than by boat or horse (rudimentary telegraphs did exist in the south of England but were reserved for the use of the navy) the new officers relied on copious correspondence to raise problems, receive new instructions and keep up to date with what was happening in Whitehall. But there was a problem. Mann had no official means of handling mail. The royal mail had been opened to commoners in 1635 by Charles I; twenty-two years later Oliver Cromwell established the General Post Office. A century after that an official post office had not been thought necessary on Mann and mail was carried to and from the island by private carriers, rather like couriers today. For two years the new island administrators put up with *ad hoc* arrangements for contacting their masters in London and probably complained vociferously about it. In 1767 an Act of Parliament was passed in Westminster to establish a postal rate for mail going to and from Mann, and organise an official packet boat from Whitehaven to Douglas to carry it.

Loss of executive power was not the least of Tynwald's difficulties. By removing the legislative function to Westminster the island no longer had the mechanism for raising revenue to fund the maintenance of insular infrastructure. The Manx could no longer raise money to finance for example repairing the island's roads, maintaining the harbours, dealing with criminals and feeding the poor. To get round the problem Tynwald created a number of boards, each to deal with a different topic, and gave them the authority to raise funding through the rates. Such statutory boards as Agriculture and Fisheries, Highways and Transport, and Education are a legacy of eighteenth century need and still act as government agencies today.

Growth of industry

One benefit the Isle of Man did glean from the Revestment Act was the removal of duties on Manx goods imported to the rest of Britain. Manufactured goods therefore became much more profitable to produce and the Manx quickly developed suitable industries to take advantage of the removal of border taxation.

Some industrial work had been conducted on Mann since the Iron Age and probably even earlier (see chapter 2), but it was the late eighteenth and nineteenth centuries which saw it mushroom. Probably the most famous industrial site on the island is the Great Laxey Mine with its iconic waterwheel named Lady Isabella after the wife of the island's Lieutenant Governor Hope. In fact the Great Laxey Mine is one of the later Manx mines, being sunk around 1780 and producing zinc, lead and copper. By that date three of the Foxdale group of lead and silver mines, Upper Old Foxdale, Lower Old Foxdale and Old Flappy had been

The Great Laxey Wheel or Lady Isabella. The largest water wheel in the world, it was designed by Manxman Robert Casement

Snaefell Mine. A lead, silver and zinc mine it closed in the early twentieth century, although its slag heaps were reworked in the 1950s for traces of uranium

operational for over forty years, while the copper mines at Bradda Head and Glen Chass were working in the seventeenth century and that at Rushen since the beginning of the eighteenth. Many lead mines also contain silver. If they contain enough, i.e. more than sixty ounces of silver per ton of lead, then until 1688 they were nominated 'royal mines' and belonged to the crown. Even after that date the mine owners had to pay duties on any precious metal ore. Some of the Manx mines came close to being royal mines, but never produced enough silver to warrant the designation. Or so their owners claimed.

The fishing industry, until recently so central to the Manx economy, benefited indirectly from the rapid increase in mining as many harbours were improved in order to be able to load and transport the mineral ore. The construction of a harbour at Laxey can be dated to about 1791 when a petition was submitted to the commissioners for the construction of a short quay on the south side of the river (roughly where the promenade ends today). The community at Laxey considered a harbour essential not only because twenty herring boats fished out of the bay, but also because the mines needed to be able to import machinery and export ore. Even with the new harbours some tasks were beyond standard harbour equipment. As late as the 1850s some of the castings for the new Lady Isabella waterwheel had to be brought into Laxey at high tide lowered over the side of the cargo ship into the sea and then retrieved from the beach after the tide had gone out.

Of course, the Revestment Act, having made smuggling illegal on the Isle of Man, actually encouraged its growth. Families not actively involved in the trade connived at any opportunity to resist the laws of their new rulers. Uniquely, one of the vessels purpose-built for the Manx smuggling trade survives. *Peggy* was built for George Quayle in 1789 by W.S. Yarwood Ltd. of Northwich, and possibly named after Quayle's mother. Originally designed for fast rowing and sailing she was later adapted to be purely a sailing boat and also appears to have been armed with small cannon. She was fitted

Cross Vein, nicknamed Snuff the Wind. One of the lead mines of the Glen Rushen group which closed in 1911

94

Laxey Harbour. Now much enlarged, the first harbour was built to serve the Laxey mines as much as the fishing fleet. The large building on the left was a warehouse for the Laxey mine

with a sliding keel, often called a drop keel – a new invention at the time – which, when down, prevents sideways movement but which, when retracted, makes the boat easy to bring close to shore. It also has the advantage of enabling small boats to carry more sail and so make them faster. Officially a mixed cargo and passenger boat, there's little doubt that *Peggy's* primary role was as a smuggling vessel.

In the five years 1789 to 1793 George Quayle had two other boats as well as the *Peggy* built. Less than ten years later, in 1802, the family opened the Isle of Man's first bank. Business must have been good. The bank was run from the family home of Bridge House in Castletown, still then considered the island's premier town. In 1935 *Peggy* was discovered walled up in the cellar of Bridge House where she had slept undisturbed for over a hundred years. Quayle was rich enough and prominent enough even to risk irritating the island's lieutenant governor. In 1809 Quayle was planning to extend Bridge House when he heard that the Lieutenant Governor was also extending Government House, now Lorne House. The governor's new extension would have enabled him to overlook Bridge House, irritating from a personal point of view and a disaster if you happen to be involved in illegal activities. The Quayles protested and were ignored, so George extended upwards instead of outwards, blocking the view from Government House of Castletown Bay and also ruining official banquets and floral decorations; the Bridge House extension prevented much sunlight reaching the governor's greenhouses.

Probably the least well known of the major Manx industries of the eighteenth and nineteenth centuries is that of linen production. It had been a small cottage industry in the early eighteenth century mostly carried on at farmhouses such as Port-e-Chee just outside Douglas. The industry had grown in importance as linen had grown to be a valuable export. Produced from the flax plant linen was bleached using buttermilk and chlorine at first, and later diluted sulphuric

acid. Bleaching in particular needed a constant supply of water – no problem on Mann – and lots of land on which to dry the bleached fabric in the sun. An important use of flax is in the manufacture of sailcloth and the Tromode Sailcloth Works of W.F. Moore & Son came into operation in 1790. Owned by the same family for the whole of its ex-

Bridge House, Castletown. Owned by the Quayle family and a centre for smuggling operations in the eighteenth century. The archway in the water beneath the blue sign is where the Peggy was concealed

istence and finally by A.W. Moore Speaker of the House of Keys and noted historian it eventually closed in 1906.

The 3rd Duke of Atholl may have been forced to sell Mann, but he still held manorial and other rights on the island and was instrumental in encouraging the linen trade. He paid much of the cost of the flax seed distributed by the Manx Society and also gave wheels for spinning flax to the poor. As a result exports of linen rose by a staggering 733% in just two years, from 12,000 yards in 1765 to at least 100,000 yards in 1767. His son, the 4th Duke, also John Murray, succeeded to the title in 1774 and even purchased the Port-e-Chee farmhouse, although he is more famous for building a sea-front residence for himself in Douglas; Castle Mona. The Duke loaned Port-e-Chee to his relative Lord Henry Murray who promptly

Lorne House, previously Government House and the residence of the Lieutenant Governor. Now privately owned

refused to move out when the duke wanted to stay there in 1793. When at last Henry was persuaded to leave the farmhouse, he took most of its contents with him.

Smaller industries making items for local use as well as for export also existed of course. They included brickworks at Castletown, Andreas and West Craig, starch making at Sulby, tanneries and bark mills including one behind Glentrammon House, papermaking at a number of sites including Laxey and Ballamillaghyn, and lime burning for agricultural use with kilns at sites including Billown and Port St Mary. Even today the half-way station on the Groudle Glen Railway is called Lime Kiln Halt. Possibly the most famous of the smaller industries and one of the few still remaining is St George's Woollen Mill at Laxey, founded by the pre-Raphaelite sympathiser John Ruskin in 1881 and now the only centre of hand weaving on the island.

The Atholls are back

John Murray the 3rd Duke of Atholl might have been induced to sell the island to the English crown, but his son didn't feel the matter ended there. The family had retained certain rights on the island (see chapter 6) but the 4th Duke felt that Mann had been sold too cheaply and wanted compensation. To that end he pestered both the British Government and King George III and eventually nagged them into appointing a Royal Commission to enquire into his claims. In 1792 the Commission produced a detailed and very long report on the economic state of the island which eventually concluded that the Duke had a point. Since the Revestment Act the Isle of Man had been under the administration of a series of governors and lieutenant governors appointed by Westminster. In an effort to reconcile the matter, in 1793 the British Government appointed John Murray, 4th Duke of Atholl as governor to the island his family once ruled.

Port-e-Chee Farmhouse west of Douglas and north of the river Glass

The Manx reception of the Duke of Atholl appears to be mixed. On the one hand they deeply resented being ruled impersonally from Westminster where island concerns were discounted, on the other they were wary of their island becoming again the domain of a single (and foreign) ruler. They also had some experience of the tendency of the Atholl family to be absentee rulers and saw that as a mixed blessing.

The Keys at this time were an unelected body, or at least unelected by anyone other than themselves. Vacancies could occur by a member dying, voluntarily giving up his office or, in extreme cases, being removed from his post by the other Keys but there was no limit to the term of office and no popular elections. The Keys were in fact something like an oligarchy of senior Manx families. For nearly 150 years from 1750 to 1898, for example, Speakers of the

Cronkbourne Village. The only industrial village on Mann it housed Irish linen workers, imported for their skills. The plaque says that designer and craftsman Archibald Knox was born here in 1864

House of Keys were members by blood or marriage of either the Moore or Taubman families.

Castle Mona c.1920. Completed in 1804 it was the seaside residence of the 4th Duke of Atholl, and originally surrounded by landscaped gardens. It soon became a hotel. but closed in 2006. At the time of writing the building is empty

To qualify to be one of the Twenty Four a candidate had to be male, over twenty one and hold landed property to a certain value per annum (see also chapter 5). The leader of the Keys was called Chairman until 1758 when George Moore on his appointment as chairman preferred instead the title of Speaker in emulation of the Westminster parliament. Vacancies among the Twenty Four were filled by the other Keys deciding on two suitable candidates whom the Speaker then presented to the island's governor for him to choose one of them. It was no surprise when, advised by the Speaker, the governor chose the one favoured by the Keys. Perhaps oddly membership of the Keys was not restricted to those who lived on Mann. John Christian Curwen, for example, although descended from one of the leading Manx families, lived mainly at Workington Hall, Cumbria. At the end of the eighteenth and beginning of the nineteenth century he was both MP for West Cumberland and a Member of the House of Keys.

At the time of the 4th Duke's search for additional compensation, the Twenty Four had

St George's Woollen Mill more commonly known as Laxey Woollen Mill

no real home of their own. Official meetings of the Keys had been held in Castle Rushen or even in one of the member's houses, but from 1710 the Keys had regularly met in the lower storey of the library built in Castletown by Bishop Wilson. By the end of the century the building had fallen into such a state of disrepair that the 1792 Royal Commission – the same one which reported in favour of additional compensation for the 4th Duke – stated it to be a 'mean, decayed building.' The Keys needed a new and permanent home but still nothing was settled for almost twenty years. Under the Revestment Act the Twenty Four had no means of raising revenue, remember. Eventually, in 1817, the Keys resolved that the building was 'not only unfit, but imminently unsafe for holding their meetings, and that they should forthwith adjourn to the George Inn'!

The Duke of Atholl was already in discussion with an architect about a building for the Keys, but there were arguments about who should pay for it. The British Government didn't see why it should pay for a meeting chamber for a body it would prefer to be without, while the Keys contested that the cost should be paid out of revenues gained from Mann. Eventually the two sides compromised with each paying part of the costs, and the go-ahead was finally given on 31 May 1819. The House of Keys building in Castletown was completed in 1821, twenty-nine years after it was first deemed necessary.

Cutting the final ties

By the late eighteenth century therefore, the island's administration was divided between the unelected Keys who tended to treat their office as a club to benefit the leading families, and the equally unelected governor and his staff who had been appointed by what many of the Manx considered a foreign power. There was some hope that the 4th Duke of Atholl would assist the Manx, not least because under the Revestment Act he retained much patronage on Mann and some of his income was still derived from the island. Unfortunately his habit of nepotism made him increasingly unpopular as he filled vacant Manx posts with his own Scottish dependents. The Duke had, for example, appointed in succession two of his brothers and a nephew as Rector of Andreas and Archdeacon of Mann. Lord George Murray took the post in 1787, Lord Charles Aynsley in 1803 and a different George Murray in 1808. The latter was only twenty four and extremely young for ordination.

The Old House of Keys, Castletown

Worse was to come. Claudius Crigan, Bishop of Sodor and Man died on 5 April 1813 and the Duke wanted to appoint the George Murray who was his nephew to the vacant see. The young man was only twenty nine and at that time Rector of Andreas. The minimum age for a bishop was thirty, so the see was left vacant for a year. He became Bishop of Sodor and Man in 1814, just as he was of an age to hold it.

Once again Mann was being treated as an absentee ruler's private fiefdom and the Manx didn't like it. The Duke's disagreements with the Keys might possibly have been shrugged off, as the Twenty Four themselves were in many respects resented and disliked for their apparent unwillingness to help the ordinary Manx. However the Duke was also insensitive to the Manx people's struggle against high taxation at a time of poor harvests. Not only was the harvest poor on land; in the early nineteenth century the Herring fishing, long seminal to the Manx economy suffered a serious downturn. The Duke ruined any chance he had of gaining popular support when he increased the island's custom duties and supported the Bishop's attempt to impose a tithe on green crops such as potatoes. The tension was exacerbated when, despite the hunger on the island, Manx landowners, many of whom were from families with members in the House of Keys, continued to export wheat as they could obtain better prices for it elsewhere. Starving people rioted and it was only an embargo placed on the export of wheat by the English-appointed Lieutenant Governor Cornelius Smelt which calmed matters down and kept people fed.

The English, Emigration and Entrepreneurs

The riots were not entirely the Duke's fault. He had spent too long away from the island and at first misunderstood the situation, but eventually ensured that some grain from overseas was imported in an endeavour to feed the Manx people. Nevertheless preventing such civil unrest was the duty of the island governor and in this he had obviously failed. As the Duke had been agitating for greater compensation for the loss of rights sold by his parents the British Government passed acts in 1824 and 1825 to purchase all the Duke's remaining manorial rights in the Isle of Man and pay him an annuity to compensate him for the future loss of duties, customs and sovereign rights. After much wrangling over the valuation the 4th Duke of Atholl sold his remaining rights for £417,144. He left the island in 1826, payment was completed in 1829 and his governorship ceased with his death in 1830. The last tie with the family which had governed the Isle of Man almost without a break for over four hundred years was finally severed.

Never to return

The Smelt Monument, Castletown. General Cornelius Smelt was a popular governor and the Doric column was to have been topped by a statue. Unfortunately the money ran out...

The Atholl family were not the only people leaving Mann, although other families were driven by need rather than greed. Even eked out by fishing and mining, the family holding was often insufficient to support all the children and the younger ones, i.e. those least likely to inherit, moved across the water in search of work. Emigration had always been a fact of life for the Manx and islanders had sailed with the Pilgrim Fathers, worked in India and settled in places as far afield as Canada, Australia and Tasmania. In the early nineteenth century the trickle of emigration became a flood as poor harvests, rising prices and the lack of work elsewhere put many small farmers out of business. There was no insular poor relief as such, and those in need relied on the church and the kindness of individuals. Emigration was often the only way to avoid starvation.

Later in the century the closure of Manx mines caused another wave of emigration as miners

left the island to seek work in the goldfields of South Africa and Australia, and various parts of North America. Thomas Kelly, a Jurby crofter, wrote in his diary on 5 July – Tynwald Day – 1827: 'This morning

Deserted tholtan, Dolland. The very real fear of starvation drove many Manx to emigrate

A Brief History of the Isle of Man

before daylight I stole away to St Johns for to see one last time the ancient ceremonies on Tynwald Hill, and secretly to take from its lowest round one little handful of that earth which has seen, maybe and heard more history than any other spot on the Island.' The following day Kelly took ship for America.

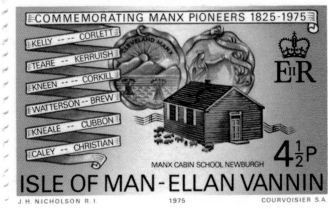

Manx emigrants. A commemorative stamp from 1975 listing Manx pioneers in Cleveland, Ohio

Particularly hard hit by the downturn in the economy were the towns. Douglas, Ramsey, Peel and Castletown had been growing slowly but steadily over the last half century. As the towns grew the health of their inhabitants declined. Houses had been built higgledy piggledy wherever seemed convenient and although by the beginning of the nineteenth century some effort was being made at urban planning, particularly in Douglas, towns were still cramped and insanitary. Although by no means free from disease, their agricultural life-style tended to hamper infection between isolated rural communities and the Manx had been largely spared the huge population losses caused by the major killer diseases such as plague, measles and smallpox experienced across the water (see chapter 4). Insanitary, crowded living conditions,

Cholera gravestone in St George's churchyard, Douglas. It marks the resting place of Matthias Kelly but also, unusually, describes the epidemic. More than 120 people died in Douglas alone and are buried in an unmarked mass grave

particularly combined with near starvation, are excellent breeding grounds for disease however and epidemics were the result.

One of the worst killers was cholera which arrived on the island from Liverpool in 1832 and caused major outbreaks in that and the following year. Cholera is a bacterial water-born disease which, unless treated, kills around half of the people it infects. Its victims die of dehydration as the disease causes sufferers to lose bodily fluids very quickly. Violent vomiting and purging usually lasts no more than twenty-four hours after which the victim is either dead or slowly recovering. Contamination can be prevented by heat or acid and infected dwellings were often disinfected with chloride of lime; when mixed with water and used as a cleaning agent it releases chlorine, which kills the cholera and a lot more besides. Other acids such as vitriol or vinegar were also occasionally used; vinegar in particular was used by nurses as a hand cleaner.

Piped water was scarce until the middle of the nineteenth century and most people relied on wells or water carts bringing supplies in from the country. Wells could be contaminated by seepage from middens while unscrupulous carters filled their barrels from the rivers, which were not only used as a general sewer, but in which infected linen was often washed. Large numbers of people died, and there was general panic. The speed of the epidemic, the circulation of the death cart collecting corpses, mass graves and the increasing fear of infection were new in Manx experience and prompted Tynwald to authorise a private company to provide the first public water supply on the island. Mann's first reservoir was at Summer Hill and supplied the growing town of Douglas

Tower of Refuge. Has any emergency shelter been quite so picturesque?

Safety from the Sea

Despite poor harvests and epidemics the early nineteenth century was not all doom and gloom. William Hillary moved to Mann in 1808, partly to escape creditors and partly because he had eloped and contracted a marriage that may well have been bigamous. He lived in Fort Anne, a large house on Douglas headland, and had excellent views of the treacherous Irish Sea. At the beginning of the nineteenth century, the Isle of Man had no lighthouses apart from a harbour light built on Douglas Pier by the harbour trustees. Frequent requests for lighthouses to protect shipping had gone unheeded and it was not until 1817 that the first lighthouse on Mann, at Point of Ayre, was designed by Robert Stevenson and built by his employers, the Commissioners of Northern Lighthouses.

The rest of the Manx coast was as yet unprotected and William Hillary was instrumental in founding what is now the Royal National Lifeboat Institute. He took part in a number of daring rescues, realising from experience that even sailors washed overboard within Douglas Bay could find the shore too far and the currents too treacherous to be saved by swimming.

Top: statue of William Hillary on Douglas Head. He looks out over his Tower of Refuge from close to where he once lived in Fort Anne. In the background is the camera obscura.
Above: the Ramsey Lifeboat coming ashore

The islet known variously as Conister Rocks or St Mary's Isle is part of a reef submerged at high tide, and had been a perennial danger to shipping. Hillary urged that a lighthouse or sanctuary be built on the islet so that shipping could be warned away, or at the very least sailors who came to grief would have somewhere safe to wait out the storm. The Harbour Commissioners mumbled about the islet being in private ownership so Hillary acted on his own, launched an appeal for public funds

A Brief History of the Isle of Man

and promised to fund any shortfall himself. Sixty-three subscribers donated cash, the Commissioners of Isle of Man Harbours also chipped in, and the Manx Attorney General John Quane, owner of St Mary's Isle, presented it to Sir William in support of his project – which was one in the eye for those who'd said that private ownership was a bar to such an edifice. Hillary himself ended up paying just under a third of the costs.

Lighthouses, Point of Ayre. The large lighthouse was the first built on Mann and showed light in 1819; the minor light and fog signal were added in 1890

Completed in 1832 the Tower of Refuge offered stranded sailors rough shelter from storms, had a bell with which to summon help and, in its early years, was kept supplied with fresh food and water. It was designed by John Welch and modelled on a romantic idea of a thirteenth century castle. Since the tower has been built, no ship has been wrecked on Conister Rocks, presumably because the tower gives a very clear indication of where they are!

Welch was busy during the first years of the 1830s. Not only did he design the Tower of Refuge but, as assistant to his brother, he'd been involved in the transformation of Castle Mona into a hotel, and had designed Ballaugh New Church and St Barnabas, Douglas too. Edward Welch was the partner of Joseph Hansom – he who designed the Hansom cab – and had arrived in the island in 1830 to design a more important building even than the Tower of Refuge. King William's College.

The school, the bishop, and the king

Bishop Barrow began it all over 150 years earlier when funds from the farming estates of Ballagilley and Hango Hill were put in trust to support two scholars training for the ministry at Trinity College Dublin (see chapter 6). Quite how a trust designed to train Manx boys for the priesthood came to be used to fund a public school many of the pupils of which have no connexion with Mann is debatable. The fact remains however that pupils of King William's College are known as Barrovians.

The sum accumulated in Bishop Barrow's Trust paid for about half the necessary work and the rest of the money was raised by an Act of Tynwald which mortgaged the estate. Funds for building the college chapel were raised in England by Bishop Ward. (Incidentally, in the late 1830s, it was Bishop Ward who led the opposition to merging the diocese of Sodor and Man with that of Carlisle.) Some brave souls approached King William IV for help with funding the college and the king is reputed to have replied that he offered 'my most valuable possession, my name'. The founders may well have been intending to name the college after Bishop Barrow but it's always difficult to refuse royalty and King William's College the new school became. It opened on 1 August 1833 with 46 pupils. One of its early pupils was the Manx poet, T.E. Brown, who was a pupil in 1845 and returned the college as vice-principal in 1855, aged only 25.

King William's College looking west from Hango Hill

The building was designed by Welch and Hansom – that's E. not J. Welch – and work began in 1830. Edward Welch left the island before the college was completed, possibly to answer questions about the builders appointed to build Birmingham Town Hall which the partnership had also designed, and John Welch always claimed to have remodelled the college tower. Whether he did or not the current tower is different again as much of the original building was destroyed by fire in 1844.

Turning the Keys to democracy

An Act of Tynwald was needed to make it possible for Bishop Barrow's Trust to be used to fund King William's College. Despite its emasculation by Westminster, Tynwald still held an important place in island affairs. The Manx had never lost their dislike of being governed by remote control – who would? – and had continued to lobby for greater self-determination. The wish to have more of a say in their own affairs was not limited to Tynwald however. If the Keys didn't like bowing to the will of Westminster, the Manx people increasingly disliked being subject to the will of the Keys.

In 1832 the British parliament passed the Reform Act which greatly increased the number of people who could vote and which, for the first time, gave voters much more of a say in who represented them in Westminster. The Manx, of course, had no Westminster MP to represent them, and no say in who became one of the Twenty Four. Possibly exacerbated by the increased enfranchisement they saw happening across the water, the Manx grew more vociferous for a similar democratic process to be applied to the Keys.

The campaign was led by two newspaper editors, Robert Fargher of *Mona's Herald*, and James Brown of *The Isle of Man Times*. Fargher was a Manxman, Brown was not, and they were rivals for readership, but they were united in their wish to see Members of the House of Keys democratically elected. At different times both were incarcerated in Castle Rushen for heaping opprobrium on the Keys as an unrepresentative oligarchy. Fargher referred to the Twenty Four as irresponsible and urged Manxmen to elect a substitute representative house, while Brown went as far as calling them Don-Keys.

The breaking point came when Brown was summoned to appear before the Keys to answer charges of libel and, instead of explaining or apologising, proceeded to say in person to the Twenty Four what he had previously said in print. He was sentenced to six months imprisonment for contempt of court – the legislature's formal designation is the Court of Tynwald (see chapter 3) – and incarcerated in Castle Rushen. Undaunted Brown continued to rage from his cell against the Keys as undemocratic political dynasties. He, or possibly his son, also applied to the Queen's Bench in London, one of the three divisions of the High Court and the one dealing with civil matters, for a writ of Habeas Corpus. Such a writ secures the release of someone who has been unlawfully detained.

The legality or otherwise of Brown's incarceration depended on the judge's interpretation of the two-fold nature of the House of Keys. He argued that 'the House of Keys sat at certain times as an Appellate Court to try cases, and at other times as a Legislative Assembly to enact laws; that as they were sitting in the latter capacity when the alleged contempt was committed, they had no power of committal…' An account at the time states: 'in less than seven weeks he was again free, and was brought down in triumph to Douglas by a large number of persons.' Unfortunately the account cannot be said to be objective as it was published, among other places, in *Brown's Popular Guide to the Isle of Man*. And, yes, the publisher was the same James Brown. He'd been released, but release was not enough, and he sued for and was awarded substantial damages.

Behind this public war of words, a new governor had been appointed to the island. Henry Brougham Loch arrived on Mann in 1863 and, like his predecessor Francis Stainsby-Conant-Pigott (lieutenant governor from 1860) dwelt in Douglas rather than in Castletown. Pigott leased Villa Marina but Loch preferred Bemahague and leased it from the trustees of Francis Daly, who was a minor, and whose mother had been the daughter of Deemster John Joseph Haywood. Bemahague was the former home of Hester (Nessy) Heywood, sister to naval officer Peter Haywood. When he was only seventeen he had been midshipman on board *HMS Bounty* at the time of the mutiny. After working tirelessly for three years Nessy was instrumental in getting her brother cleared of complicity. Bemahague never returned to the Daly family, being leased to the governor until purchased in 1903, when the governor was Lord Raglan. Today it is known as Government House.

Government House. Formerly known as Bemahague, it was the home of Elisabeth Betham, daughter of a customs collector stationed in Douglas. She married Cornishman William Bligh of Bounty fame

Governor Loch very quickly noticed that the island needed some way to raise funds to repair its own infrastructure and was particularly concerned about the protection of Douglas Harbour. Westminster had already made clear that it was unwilling to hand the control of taxes paid by the people to a body not chosen by the people. If the Keys wanted to control the pursestrings therefore, they themselves needed to be subject to control through the ballot box. The James Brown debacle merely made more urgent the solution of a problem which Governor Loch was already considering.

A trickle of Acts passed by Westminster during the decade or so preceding 1866, many of them concerned with refurbishing harbours, had emphasised the need for reform. Governor Loch undertook a series of delicate negotiations, on the one side with the Twenty Four urging them to vote themselves out of a job, and on the other with Westminster urging it to renounce control of much of the Manx revenue. 1866 was a momentous year for Manx government. Almost exactly a century after the Revestment Act ended Tynwald's control of Manx revenue, the Isle of Man, Customs, Harbours and Public Purposes Act was passed by Westminster returning control of revenue raised from the island to the island. The only exception was £10,000 per annum which the British Government retained for providing naval and military protection. In the same year the House of Keys Election Act was passed by Tynwald ending the oligarchic nature of the Keys and providing for public elections.

The island was divided into ten electoral districts. The sheadings of Glenfaba, Michael, Ayre, Garff, Middle and Rushen elected three members each as did the town of Douglas. The towns of Peel, Ramsey and Castletown each elected one member. Only men who owned real estate valued at not less than eight pounds, or tenants paying an annual rent of not less than twelve pounds were allowed to vote. Reluctant some of the Keys might initially have

been to make their position subject to democratic election, but within twenty years the Twenty Four went from unelected body to pioneers of democracy. The Election Act passed by the Keys in 1881 extended the right to vote in various ways not least opening the franchise to spinsters or widows who owned property. The Keys led the world in recognising that its members represented taxpayers regardless of their sex. New Zealand is usually quoted as the first country in the world to recognise female suffrage in its elections of 1893. In fact the Isle of Man granted women the vote twelve years earlier.

The focus of the island was moving towards Douglas. By the last half of the nineteenth century, it was by far the biggest town, most of the island's legitimate trade was conducted through its docks and harbour, and Governor Loch had elected to live there. It made no sense for the island parliament to be situated in Castletown, ten miles away from what was becoming the nerve centre of Mann. The Keys needed to move, and they needed suitable premises to move to.

The Bank of Mona building is now home to the House of Keys. Painted white for many years, the building was originally red to match the Legislative Building next door. Public opinion wanted the white retained when the building was restored in 2004

At first they took up residence in the Douglas Court House, but were searching for somewhere with more room when the Bank of Mona closed (see below). The Bank of Mona's building in Douglas had been built in 1855 to the design of John Robinson, who also designed what is now Falcon Cliff Court – the white building with the single turret which stands above the Central Promenade – for its manager. On 7 November 1879 it was purchased by the Keys as their new home. Fittingly their former home became the Castletown branch of Dumbell's Bank – of which more anon.

Holiday hot spot

The need for repairs to the harbours, particularly that of Douglas was one of the reasons prompting Governor Loch to seek ways whereby the Manx could again be responsible for their own island, and it was not only for reasons of trade. Since the 1830s the island had attracted increasing numbers of visitors and, by the last quarter of the nineteenth century, tourism was making a significant contribution to the Manx economy. In the textile towns of the north of England, the idea of a week-long holiday, albeit unpaid, was becoming the norm. As it was more cost effective to close the mill rather than have serial absences, it became usual for all the mills in one area to close together in a holiday known as Wakes Week. Those who worked together often played together and whole communities travelled to the Isle of Man for fun and relaxation. Mann was the holiday destination of choice in the late nineteenth century, just as Spain was for many late twentieth century holiday-makers.

The Cunningham camp c.1910. The large building is the dining pavilion

Considered exotic, yet reasonably easy to get to, the island infrastructure was transformed by the need to cater for its visitors, and part them from their cash.

The most pressing requirement for the increasing numbers of visitors was of course somewhere to stay. Hotels had not been much needed on Mann before the nineteenth century. If Manx residents went to visit friends and neighbours, distances were either short enough for there to be no need to stay overnight, or they stayed with those they were visiting. Only really Douglas offered purchasable overnight accommodation, and that was often dubious and designed to serve the needs of sailors working on the trading ships. Consequently the island experienced a major building boom.

Many of the hotels and former hotels along the Douglas sea front date from the end of the nineteenth century. The sea front was originally Sand Street, later renamed Strand Street, and the Loch Promenade together with its crescent of hotels was built on land reclaimed from the sea; it was further widened and more land reclaimed in 1933. Other Manx towns also expanded. Promenades was built at Port Erin and Port St Mary and the Mooragh Promenade in Ramsey was begun but not completed. Only Peel and Castletown remained relatively unaltered by tourism.

Accommodation to serve every need – and purse – quickly flourished. Gentleman's residences such as Fort Anne were converted to top-grade hotels, but many more were purposely-built ranging from the Villiers, the largest hotel on the island with upwards of three hundred rooms, through family-run boarding houses to Cunningham's Young Men's Holiday Camp where 'clean living young men' found cheap holidays under canvas. The first holiday camp in the world was opened at Howstrake in 1894 by Joseph Cunningham a Liverpool flour trader, baker and staunch Presbyterian. It could accommodate 600 young men. Ten years later the camp moved to Victoria Road, Douglas, just to the east of what is now Noble's Park and the Howstrake site continued to operate under different hands. Living quarters on the new site were a mix of tents and chalets accommodating nearly 4,000. The camp had its own shops, swimming pool, playing fields, a bank and was virtually self sufficient in food; Joseph Cunningham purchased Ellerslie Manor (see chapter 3) in 1898 and developed it as a model farm supplying produce to feed his holidaymakers.

Cunningham supplied many entertainments for his guests, but others were developing their own properties to attract the tourists. Riversdale, a couple of miles west of Laxey, became a restaurant and place of entertainment for visitors to Glen Roy around the 1850s, for example. The upper part of the glen was laid out with footpaths and seats and a small charge made for entry. Port Erin had a swimming pool at Spaldrick, while Douglas installed a camera obscura on Douglas Head, Ramsey had its salt baths and Glen Helen its Swiss Cottage. A popular pleasure resort was the grounds of Injebreck House, north of the Injebreck or West Baldwin reservoir. According to its advertisements the resort included: 'magnificent pavilion for dancing; longest switchback railway; largest pleasure resort on the island with 700 acres of

Manx Electric Railway car 22 and trailer 44 passing Crowcreen southbound

A Brief History of the Isle of Man

beautiful glens, plantation, gardens and forests; miniature grand orchestra; promenade concerts and a sacred concert each Sunday in the season.'

Many of the attractions, including most of the glens, were owned by the railway companies, an entrepreneurial business venture unusual in British railways at the time. In the tourist industry the Isle of Man was proving itself to be something of a pioneer, with attractions integrated with the transport which served them, the first holiday camp and almost the first electric railway to serve it. When it was built in 1893, the electric tram system used state-of-the-art technology imported from America. It was one of the first electric tramways in Britain and pre-dates many of the roads on the Manx north east coast. Originally built as part of the planned development of the Howstrake estate it terminated at Groudle where a new hotel had been built. The glen was being developed as a pleasure attraction and by 1896 even had its own small zoo and miniature steam railway. Meanwhile the success of the electric railway led to it being extended to Laxey and a through service to Ramsey introduced for the 1899 season.

Isle of Man railway locomotive Loch, named after the mid-nineteenth century governor. The train is at Keristal en route to Port Erin

As wheeled traffic came late to the island (see chapter 6), roads on Mann were in general poor, so railways offered a welcome possibility for inland travel. The first line to open was from Douglas to Peel in 1873, followed by the line from Douglas to Port Erin the following year. The Manx Northern line opened from St John's to Ramsey in 1879 and the line from St John's to Foxdale in 1886. Within less than fifteen years therefore, the Isle of Man went from having no railways at all, to lines serving all its main towns, and many of its smaller ones. It's even more startling to think that the whole of the Manx railway system was installed in the twenty-three years between 1873 and 1896.

As well as various cliff railways, and utility railways such as the Douglas Horse Tramway and the tiny electric tramway on the Queen's Pier Ramsey, several Manx tramways were built

purely for tourists. The most famous of these is undoubtedly the Snaefell Mountain Railway, which opened in 1895 and provided tourists who were not good walkers with the ability to visit the highest point on the island. The same year saw the opening of an even more spectacular tourist tramway, the Douglas Southern

Entrance to the Marine Drive. Apart from fugitive traces, only the arch now remains of the spectacular ride to Port Soderick

Electric Tramway, which transported tourists along the newly constructed Marine Drive around the coast south of Douglas to Port Soderick; it included three overbridges, two of them across sea coves.

The last of the Manx transport systems to be installed was the Upper Douglas Cable Tramway in 1896. The horse tramway had meant that island visitors could be met from their boat and taken, with their luggage, along the promenade to wherever they were staying. The hotels and boarding houses on the higher levels were losing business and wanting to be served by similarly modern and convenient public transport. A tramway using conventional overhead cables was not feasible because of the steepness of the gradients, so a cable tramway was installed. The trams in such a system have no motive power of their own but grip a moving cable set beneath the road surface and are hauled along or stop as the driver operates the grippers to seize or release the cable. Trams in San Francisco work on the same principle today, and the Douglas tramway in fact utilised the experience of cable traction gained from the San Francisco system. The Upper Douglas Cable Tramway ran from Victoria Street, up Prospect Hill and along Bucks, Woodbourne, York and Ballaquayle Roads before descending to

Loch Promenade, Douglas, I.O.M.

Douglas in its holiday heyday. In the bottom left-hand corner is a rare view of one of the cable tramcars

the Villa Marina along Broadway. One of its principal supporters and financial backers was Alexander Bruce, entrepreneur, financer of the Isle of Man Tramways & Electric Power Company and, more significantly, general manager of Dumbell's Bank.

Farrago in finance

Two names stand out in Manx financial circles of the nineteenth century: Henry Bloom Noble and George William Dumbell. The former is the island's most notable philanthropist, the latter possibly its most infamous businessman, and neither were Manxmen. Noble had come to Mann with nothing, had made a fortune by trade and money lending, and when he died childless left most of his wealth, including his house, in trust to benefit those of the Manx who were poor, sick or old. Noble left his name to a hospital, park and numerous smaller projects all of them financed either by him in his lifetime or by his legacy after his death. Dumbell left his name to a row of miners' cottages in Laxey, a clock in Douglas and probably the biggest financial scandal known on the island.

The Isle of Man had often been the refuge for those across the water who were suffering financial embarrassment, as debtors could not legally be pursued there under British law.

Jonathan Dumbell, George's father, was one of the partners in the short-lived Stockport Bank and had been bankrupted by its failure in 1793 only two years after it had been established. Despite the bankruptcy Dumbell senior was not poor but, possibly to escape creditors or possibly to maximise the wealth he had left, around 1815, brought his family to Mann.

Dumbell's Row, Laxey. Built for miners in 1860 it was often called Ham and Egg Terrace as it contained a number of small eateries catering for hungry miners

In quick time George William Dumbell became a Manx advocate, purchased several properties on the island and, from 1840 to 1858, was a Member of the House of Keys in its unelected days. Within a few months of his appointment he was Secretary of the House and was also a major shareholder in the Isle of Man Joint Stock Bank. The bank failed in 1843, a presage and perhaps a warning of what was to come.

Like his father, Dumbell seems to have particularly wanted to be a banker and, when the Douglas and Isle of Man Bank run by Henry, John and James Holmes ceased trading in 1854 it was taken over by a partnership of Dumbell, Son and Howard, Dumbell's brother in law. Known always as Dumbell's, and officially so after it became a limited liability company in 1874, it experienced its first problems only three years after it opened. On 22 August 1857 a notice was posted on the front door stating: 'The bank is compelled to suspend business for the present. No doubt need be felt that everyone will be paid in full, and that speedily. George William Dumbell.'

Dumbell was helped out of the crisis by his own oratory skills and the temporary closure in November of the same year of the Bank of Mona. Dumbell's continued and, by the time of its flotation, the bank's chairman was or had been involved in many of the most significant Manx businesses, including the Manx Telegraph Company, the Great Laxey Mine and the Isle of Man Railway Company. He also owned over 870 acres of land. His great rivalry was with the Bank of Mona, which was deeply respected and more conservative than Dumbell's. It was a subsidiary of the City of Glasgow Bank and was the first bank to have branches in all four of the main Manx towns. When the Bank of Mona's parent organisation failed in 1878 the Manx division, although solvent and well managed, had also to close.

Manager of the Ramsey branch of the Bank of Mona was Alexander Bruce and, when the Bank of Mona closed, Dumbell, now aged 74, offered Bruce the job of manager in Dumbell's Banking Company. As Dumbell became more feeble with age and ill health, Bruce became more powerful. Within ten years and, just before Dumbell's death in 1887, he became General Manager.

Bruce had the instincts of a venture capitalist without the judgement. He continued the bank's policy of investment, particularly in tourism, often without either sufficient security for loans or the funds to underwrite them. He helped fund the Isle of Man Tramways & Electric Power Company and the Cable Tramway, loaned to boarding houses trying to build up the tourist trade and even became involved in a brewery syndicate. Such were the apparent profits that Bruce seemed metaphorically to be printing money. Unfortunately Dumbell's bank did print its own notes but had grossly insufficient assets to back them up.

Other banks had been suspicious for some time. In September 1890 the Douglas Town Commissioners purchased the town's water supply from the Douglas Water Company for around £146,000. The commissioners banked with Dumbell's and Bruce was Town Treasurer. The Water Company however, whose chairman was Henry Bloom Noble, banked with the Isle of Man Banking company Ltd. and refused to accept a cheque drawn on Dumbell's as payment for their assets. Douglas Water Company demanded cash and cash it was paid.

On 30 November 1899, John Curphey, head cashier of Dumbell's, resigned his position. The following day he wrote a personal letter to the Chairman stating: 'a most dangerous and critical state of the bank's affairs, brought about by years of gross neglect on the part of the managers...it is well-known to the managers themselves, the auditors and every member of the staff.' He was rewarded for his honesty by being appointed manager of a branch of the Isle of Man Banking Company Ltd.

Two months later Dumbell's bank crashed. Its obituary was written in the *Manx Sun*, which had long been criticising its soundness: 'The 3rd of February, 1900, will be a day of evil memory in "Our Island Story" for generations to come. It was on that day Dumbell's Bank, virtually the Manx National Bank, tottered to its fall, and, in its fall, spread ruin and misery far and wide.' Purple prose it might be, but the *Manx Sun* was right. The effects of the crash of Dumbell's Bank continued to be felt more than a century later. Some Manx organisations never recovered.

The Jubilee Clock at the bottom of Victoria Street on Loch Promenade, Douglas. It is one of the very few things on Mann still to bear Dumbell's name

CHAPTER 8

CHANGING EMPHASIS

Only one month into the new century and the fall of Dumbell's Bank affected not only most people on the Isle of Man but also a good number beyond it. Directly affected were the railways, particularly the electric railways which had been the brainchild of Bruce. Many of the tourist entertainment complexes, such as Derby Castle and The Palace with its enormous ballroom, both of which were in Douglas, owed their existence to the bank and their future was in doubt. A brewery syndicate including many breweries, public houses and hotels was also intrinsically connected with Dumbell's. The tourist trade was affected by the crash as boarding houses saw their capital disappear, could neither pay staff nor complete renovations and had to turn tourist business away. The Isle of Man Steam Packet Company lost thousands from its company account in the unfortunate bank and, like many, also found its profits affected. In 1900 it carried about half the freight of the previous year and fewer passengers to the island, although it did gain a small profit from those taking one-way tickets to Liverpool to escape the mess. Even food sales were affected as there were fewer people to eat it, less money to pay for it and traders saw the island as a bad risk. Thousands of small businesses and individuals lost their working capital, often representing their hard-earned savings and those not pushed into bankruptcy almost ceased trading for a while as they didn't know whose money to trust.

The new century had started badly and did not improve immediately. On 29 January 1901 Queen Victoria died. She ascended the British throne in 1837 and had reigned so long that many of her subjects could remember no other monarch. The 4th Duke of Atholl had relinquished his rights on Mann in 1826 so Queen Victoria had been Lord of Mann for almost the entire time since the Atholl/Derby reign had ended. Always conscious of her femininity Victoria preferred to be called Lady of Mann rather than Lord.

Public mourning was decently observed, but of more immediate concern to the island was the liquidation of The Isle of Man Tramways and Electric Power Company. The demise of the company affected not only public transport and tourist rides, but also part of the electricity supply to the public – the tramway provided it. As well as the electric tramway from Douglas to Ramsey (what is now the Manx Electric Railway) the company also owned the Snaefell Mountain Railway, the Douglas

Horse tram 36 with motive power unit (horse!) Charles. The crash of Dumbell's bank is the reason why the horse trams are owned by Douglas Corporation and all other public transport by the Isle of Man Government. The advert carried on the facia board is particularly appropriate

Bay Tramway (the horse trams), the Upper Douglas Cable Tramway and several commercial activities along the coastal line, including a granite quarry at Dhoon and licensed refreshment rooms and hotels. The company was sold off with Douglas Corporation purchasing the horse and cable tramways and the newly-formed Manx Electric Railway Co. Ltd. (MER) taking over everything else. That sale is the reason why those wishing to travel on the MER today have to go to the wrong end of Douglas promenade to do so. Plans first mooted in 1894 to run the electric railway to the Victoria Pier and thus near to the business heart of Douglas were shelved when Dumbell's crashed and, despite lobbying, have never been seriously reconsidered.

The MER took over control of its slice of the assets of the defunct Isle of Man Tramways and Electric Power Company on 18 August 1902. Just over a week earlier, on 9 August 1902, Victoria's son Albert Edward, was crowned King Edward VII. Mann no longer belonged to the Derby/Atholl families, but the ancient tie was still acknowledged by feudal tribute. On 28 August 1902 the *Manchester Guardian* stated: 'Among the feudal services the two falcons from the Isle of Man were conspicuous. Seated on the wrist of his Grace's hawking gauntlet, the beautiful Peregrine Falcons appeared with their usual ornaments. The birds sat perfectly tame on the arm of his Grace, completely hooded and furnished with bells. The King descended from his chair of state, and the ladies of the Court pressed round to caress and examine the noble birds.'

Albert Tower, Ramsey. It was built to mark the point to which Queen Victoria's consort climbed to admire the view

The coronation was originally planned for June, but the crown prince developed appendicitis two days beforehand, needed an operation and the ceremony was postponed. The King, convalescing aboard the royal yacht after the strain of the coronation, paid a surprise visit to the Isle of Man rather as his parents had done fifty-five years before. At that time Queen Victoria had stayed aboard the royal yacht but Prince Albert came ashore and asked the first man he met, who happened to be a barber, to conduct him to the top of the hill so that he could admire the view. The Albert Tower was built to commemorate his visit.

Plaque to mark the inception of the Gordon Bennett auto race. It can be found at Port-e-Vullen

Ramsey had been known as Royal Ramsey for centuries, partly because the ancient Royal Way runs from the town to Tynwald and then to Castletown. The title flourished however, with such fortuitous pieces of civic one-upmanship when it became the chosen landing place of both Prince Albert and King Edward VII. Unlike his mother, Edward came ashore and, with Queen Alexandria, visited Bishopscourt, Peel Castle, Cronkbourne House and Douglas before returning to Ramsey on the MER. The tiny Royal Saloon (No. 59) used for the occasion still exists and is sometimes used at special events.

A Brief History of the Isle of Man

The need for speed

The event most associated with the Isle of Man is undoubtedly the TT (Tourist Trophy) races. Now purely for motocycles, the first races took place in cars. James Gordon-Bennett (yes, he of the expression) owned the *New York Herald* which he managed from his yacht the *Lysistrata* on which he travelled around Europe. He established various sporting trophies including the Gordon-Bennett balloon race which still exists, and, in 1900, the Gordon-Bennett Cup for car racing. Planned as an annual race for national teams the British did not attend the first race, had only one car in the second and, by a fluke, won the third race in 1902; their man Selwyn Edge driving a Napier was the only one to finish. The winning country hosted the following year's event but no purpose-built stadia existed at the time and the Westminster parliament was reluctant to close the necessary roads. The Automobile Club of Great Britain and Ireland therefore remembered the final part of its name and took the race to Ireland for 1903.

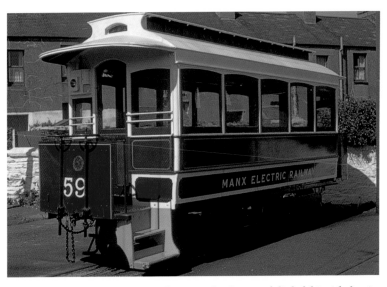

National teams had to drive cars designed and built in their country and British-made cars were inferior to those of their rivals. The problem was one of testing; the British team had nowhere to trial vehicles and see how they performed. The secretary of the Automobile Club, Julian Orde, thought of the Isle of Man. Its parliament

Royal Coach No. 59. A palace on wheels, it is delightful inside but its short wheel base gives it a very odd waddling motion!

was small – fewer people to convince – it was trying to extract itself from a major financial crisis so was looking for ways to make money, and its people were already used to welcoming myriad visitors from across the water. And of course Orde's cousin, Lord Raglan, was governor. That helped.

The necessary legislation was rushed through on 15 March 1904, the royal assent necessary for all Acts of Parliament was granted on 28 March and the trials were scheduled for 10 May. But there was a problem. For a thousand years no Manx law has taken effect before its promulgation on Tynwald Hill and Tynwald Day is 5 July, *after* the date set for the trials. Nevertheless the legislature was determined that those trials should take place on Mann so decided to hold a special Tynwald Day on 5 May to make the trials legal. All necessary personnel were transported to St John's appropriately enough by cars specially organised by Julian Orde, and the Highways (Light Locomotive) Act 1904 duly promulgated on Tynwald Hill. Most of the Keys and Legislative Council had not travelled in a motorised road vehicle before.

Wheels had only been seen on Manx roads for a couple of hundred years, so such roads were hardly ideal for racing. Often unfenced, with poor surfaces and liable to be invaded by straying animals without warning, the trails course was much longer than the current TT course, going through St Jude's and reaching as far south as Castletown. The trials were run, the British team selected, and the precedent set for road racing on the island – and encouragement incidentally provided for improving the island's roads.

The car trials were repeated in 1905, with the addition of motorbike trials for a forthcoming series of international motor cycle races. That September also saw touring cars take part in a new race called the Tourist Trophy. The Gordon-Bennett car road-racing event was replaced by the first Grand Prix motor racing event in 1906 but by that time the island was hooked. 28 May 1907 saw the first Tourist Trophy race for motorbikes on the island, held the day before the car TT. It was another fifteen years before the current circuit became the accepted course, but the annual TT event was an accepted fact.

Nationalism and home rule

Despite or possibly because of repeated invasion, whether peaceful or otherwise, the Manx were a fiercely independent people and there was a growing demand for that independence to be recognised. The Manx National Reform League was founded in 1903 to lobby for greater Manx responsibility for their own affairs plus a democratically-elected second chamber. Rather oddly, the League's elected president was not a Manxman. Thomas Henry Hall Caine was born in Runcorn, Cheshire and, although his father was Manx and Hall Caine had often stayed on the Isle of Man, he was forty-one before he moved to the island permanently. A novelist and playwright, his works were extremely popular in the late nineteenth and early twentieth century, but although sometime Member of the House of Keys (MHK) for Ramsey, he was considered a patronising poseur and generally disliked.

As well as the inauguration of the motorbike TT in 1907, the year saw another first; the introduction of the Manx National Anthem (*Arrane Ashoonagh dy Vannin*). Written by W.H. Gill and with a tune adapted from a traditional Manx air, it was sung for the first time at the 1907 Manx Music Festival in Peel. Although written and often sung in English, the Manx translation by J.J. Kneen is growing in popularity:

O Land of our birth	*O Halloo nyn ghooie,*
O gem of God's earth	*O Chliegeen ny s'bwaaie*
O Island so strong and so fair;	*Ry gheddyn er ooir aalin Yee;*
Built firm as Barrule,	*Ta dt'Ardstoyl Reill-Thie*
Thy throne of Home Rule	*Myr Baarool er ny hoie*
Makes us free as thy sweet mountain air.	*Dy reayll shin ayns seyrsnys as shee.*

Whenever the Lord of Man or his/her Lieutenant is present, the British National Anthem must be played, but *O Land of our Birth* is often played as well. Like *God Save the Queen*, the Manx National Anthem has a number of verses which are rarely used.

In 1907 the Manx might have sung of home rule, but they didn't enjoy it. The Westminster government still made or at least had to ratify all policy decisions, local taxation and expenditure were controlled by the UK Treasury, and officials were appointed by Westminster and therefore almost invariably not Manxmen. Most importantly, although the twenty-four Keys in the lower house were elected by the Manx people, the Legislative Council which formed the upper chamber of Tynwald was formed entirely of officials appointed by Westminster, plus the Lieutenant Governor. The Keys power was largely negative; they had the right to veto legislation, but couldn't introduce measures without the support of the Legislative Council, the Lieutenant Governor and, ultimately, the Westminster parliament. That situation changed during the course of the twentieth century, but several major events intervened to interrupt the process. Not least was the advent of the First World War.

Conflict

From around this time thousands of territorial soldiers were visiting the Isle of Man for summer training camps, arriving at Peel for the camp at Knockaloe Mooar Farm or Ramsey for Milntown. The latter seems an appropriate site for military training as it's very near the site of Godred Croven's decisive battle at Sky Hill in 1079 (see chapter 3). Knockaloe Camp was to have a particularly important role in the coming conflict.

1913 was a record season for visitors to the Isle of Man with nearly 616,000 people landing at Douglas and Ramsey during the summer. The entire population of the island was only around 52,000 at the time and a large proportion were working in the holiday trade. When

Graves in Patrick's churchyard of some of the internees who died during the First World War. Knockaloe Mooar Farm, where they were interned, can just be seen through the trees to the left

Britain declared war on Germany on 4 August 1914 that year's season was in full swing and few thought that the war would last more than a few months. Even so Mann, like everywhere else, was put on a war footing.

As was the case throughout most of Britain and its Empire, many Manxmen volunteered to fight, but unlike most other places in the First World War, their families and homeland were also immediately affected by the conflict. The Manx holiday trade ceased abruptly of course, but was replaced by troop movements often filling the beds previously occupied by holidaymakers. On 5 August 1914 the British government also received royal assent for the Aliens Restriction Act. By it non-British citizens were required to register with the authorities and, if deemed necessary, interned. The remoteness of the Isle of Man, its distance from Germany and, most importantly, the fact that it was surrounded by water led the British government to consider it an ideal place to intern so-called enemy aliens.

Cunningham's Holiday Camp in Victoria Road, Douglas (see chapter 7) was taken over as the first internment camp, with the first group of internees arriving on 22 September 1914. Many of the tents had been replaced by wooden huts for holidaymakers but these in turn were replaced by chalets built by the internees. The numbers interned increased rapidly and soon filled the room available for them at Douglas. Two months later the old territorial army camp at Knockaloe was transformed into an internment camp which grew and grew. Originally intended to house 5,000 internees, by the end of the war it contained around 23,000 prisoners, equivalent to almost half the normal civilian population of the island. Twenty-three compounds each capable of taking one thousand men were divided between four camps sharing the same

Cunningham's Holiday Camp. Although intended as home to tourists only in the holiday season, the huts housed internees all year round

site. Largely thanks to the organisation of the Society of Friends the camps had their own bakery, schools for adults, workshops, theatres and sports events, and the central administration even had its own railway on specially-laid tracks delivering coal and supplies from Peel.

By November 1914 four of the Isle of Man Steam Packet Boats had already been chartered or purchased by the British government for war work. The *Peel Castle*, *King Orry* and *Ramsey* were first commissioned as modern-day privateer ships, carrying light armaments and fast enough to capture and board enemy merchantmen, while the *Snaefell* formed part of the Plymouth patrol protecting the English Channel. Probably the most unusual use of a Manx ship at the time was the 1915 conversion of the *Ben-my-Chree* to a seaplane carrier. By the end of the war a total of eleven of the Packet Company's fifteen ships had seen war service. Only the *Peel Castle*, *King Orry*, *Viking* and *Mona's Queen* returned, the latter with the distinction of being probably the only paddle steamer to have sunk a German submarine by hitting it with one of her paddles. Three others were retained by the British government and four were sunk including the *Ramsey*, *Snaefell* and *Ben-my-Chree*.

Nor was the conflict a remote event. B.E. Sergeaunt in his book *The Isle of Man and the Great War* says: 'The crew of the first vessel to be sunk by a submarine in the Irish Sea was brought into Douglas on 30 January 1915, by a small collier, whose normal route lay between the Mainland and the Island; five more vessels were sunk on the following day.' Survivors were not the only ones brought to the island as the bodies of their comrades were washed ashore. Steamer communications were interrupted, planes were in their infancy and telegraph communication relied on a submarine cable coming ashore at Cornaa which was vulnerable to being cut; direct telephonic communication with England did not arrive until 1929. The Isle of Man had lost none of its strategic importance and a wireless station was installed to ensure that communication across the water was maintained throughout the war.

Loosening the shackles

One of the surprise decisions at the end of the First World War was the resignation of Lord Raglan from the post of Lieutenant Governor, a position he'd held since 1902. It might have been a shock but for many Manx it was not an unwelcome one. Lord Raglan had long stood in the way of administrative and political reform and there was hope that his successor Major General William Fry would be more sympathetic to the Manx wish for greater self-government. There was probably some hope that the poor man was henpecked; his wife was a Manxwoman and daughter to Sir John Goldie-Taubman, a former Speaker of the House of Keys.

Through no fault of its own the Isle of Man lagged behind much of the rest of Great Britain in the provision support for the old, unemployed, poor and sick. In the rest of Britain rudimentary support was introduced in 1909 for old-age pensions, 1911 for unemployment insurance and 1601 for the care of the poor and sick. The latter, the Elizabethan Poor Law, survived for over 300 years as the basis for raising money to help the destitute on a parish by parish basis, the money going to support the workhouse. The institution might have been feared and hated and have become a by-word for misery, but it did at least exist as a final resort. The Isle of Man had no governmental provision at all. Largely because Tynwald had no authority to raise money for anyone in need, support for those who could not afford to support themselves, and had no family able to help, remained purely in the hands of philanthropic individuals or organisations.

That had to change and the new Lieutenant Governor was willing to co-operate with Tynwald in its search for greater independence from Westminster control. The argument used so effectively by Governor Loch in 1866 when seeking to transform the Keys into an elected body (see chapter 7) was now applied the other way round. At that time Loch made it clear that Westminster was unwilling to hand the control of taxes paid by the people to a body not chosen by the people; now the Keys were unwilling to vote for additional taxes if Tynwald's second chamber, the Legislative Council, was not answerable to the Manx people.

In 1919 the Legislative Council adopted the Constitution Amendment Bill. Like the Keys in 1866 some members were effectively voting themselves out of

Legislative Building. Next door to the Bank of Mona building, the stained glass windows on the top floor indicate the Tynwald Chamber, where the Keys meet

a job. Ex-officio membership of the Council by the Vicar-General, the Archdeacon, and the Receiver General ceased, the motion being proposed, seconded, and supported respectively by the three members to be eliminated. In the future the Legislative Council was to be made up of four members elected by the Keys and two nominated by the Governor. Crucially, whereas previously Manx finance had been decided by the parliament in Westminster, from 1919 all future financial matters were to be discussed by both chambers. Such changes demonstrated the truth of the Manx saying *Stroshey yn theay na yn Chiarn* (the common people are stronger than the Lord of Man). From around this time the Speaker of the House of Keys began to wear a wig and gown similar to that worn by his peer the Speaker of the House of Commons, perhaps as a symbol of increasing independence and pride in his office.

The beneficial effects of the new order were felt in some quarters almost immediately. On 18 May 1920 the Old Age Pension and National Insurance Acts were passed in Tynwald. In March of that year, anticipating the Act, more than 1,000 people aged seventy and over received an old-age pension for the first time.

Flight from Mann!

After the war the Manx tourist trade increased quickly and was soon back to pre-war levels. The first aeroplane to arrive on the island came – by boat! – in 1911, but pleasure flying began in earnest after the war. In 1919 two Avro biplanes crossed from Blackpool and, for a couple of seasons gave rides around Douglas Bay using the strip of grass between the Queens' Promenade and the beach as their airfield.

It was 1928 before an aeroplane visited the island again, this time bringing freight in the form of thousands of *The Motor Cycle* magazines for visitors to the TT races. Part of the Imperial Airways fleet, the plane left Croydon, refuelled in Manchester and landed at Ronaldsway after a 4½ hour flight. The field where the plane landed belonged to a farm owned by King William's College (see chapter 7). Passenger services began in 1931 when the British Amphibious Aircraft Company began a service from Blackpool; tickets were £1.80 return. Scheduled services at £3.00

Above: Terminal buildings of Croydon airport. The aerodrome is now industrial estate and housing. Probably the first plane ever to land at Ronaldsway flew from here
Right: Ronaldsway aerodrome with a Dash 8/Q400 taking off

return from Blackpool began the following year with flying boats landing in Douglas Bay, Derbyhaven or on land at Ronaldsway. That same year William Cunningham of Holiday Camp fame became the first Manxman to own and fly his own plane.

Flying visits by Prince George, youngest son of George V and Queen Mary, and Amy Johnson and her husband followed, and travel by air was obviously growing in importance. A regular land-based service operated by Blackpool and West Coast Air Services Ltd was inaugurated for the summer season of 1933 between Mann and Blackpool and/or Liverpool. The following season flights linked the island with Manchester and Belfast.

Ronaldsway, set as it is in the far south of the Isle of Man was not convenient for those who lived in or were visiting the north of the island. A second airfield was opened in 1935 on land belonging to Close Lake Farm. Named the Hall Caine Airport in memory of the writer (see above) who died in 1931, it was partly funded by his son. United Airways used it to operate services between the island and Blackpool, Liverpool, Carlisle and Glasgow. Ronaldsway still had the larger number of flights but both airfields were operational when the development of improved flying capabilities was both stimulated and redirected by a crisis which affected not only the island but the world. The Second World War.

War again

Although war was on the cards, and recognised as being so, many tried to carry on as normal during 1938 and the summer months of 1939. Holiday makers still flocked to the island and the TT races ran in June as had become usual. Ominously the rise of Nazi Germany was apparent even during sporting events. Jimmy Guthrie six-times winner of the TT had been killed in a crash at the German Grand Prix in August 1937. A memorial to him was unveiled on the TT course the following year. Among those present was Baron von Falkenhayn, a member of a prominent German family with a strong military tradition. He laid a wreath covered with swastikas and gave the Nazi salute. Perhaps more worrying

Jurby airfield. Able still to be used if planes have to be diverted from Ronaldsway, it also hosts a variety of other events. Here the Andreas Racing Association hold a European Open Competition over the runways and taxi ways

was German strength in the air. The London to Isle of Man air race in 1937, for example, was won by Major Hans Seidemann, a German pilot flying a Messerschmitt sporting a swastika. He may have taken a menacing number of air photographs on the way.

Despite Neville Chamberlain's pronouncement on 30 September 1938 of 'peace for our time', despite the *Daily Express* headline on 7 August 1939 stating 'no war this year', everyone knew that war was coming. Flying had developed so much in the inter-war years that it played a much more significant part in the development of both the Second World War as a whole and the Isle of Man in particular. Negotiations had already taken place between Tynwald and Westminster about the creation of an RAF base on Mann in the event of another war. In 1938 work started on creating an airfield at Jurby. It was ready when war was declared in September the following year and became the No 5 Bombing and Gunnery School with Battle, Blenheim

Disused airfield near Andreas. These are some of the Second World War buildings still to survive

and Wallace aircraft at first. In 1941 Jurby was renamed No 5 Air Observer School and in 1944 Air Navigation and Bombing School. After the war the airfield became a training station and remained as an official RAF base until 1972.

It had only been two decades since the Great War and memories were still fresh of the internees at Knockaloe and Douglas, so it was little surprise to the Manx people that the island was again called on to host internees and prisoners of war. The tourist industry was of course non existent during the war and hotels stood empty. Many were requisitioned, fenced off with barbed wire and turned into internment camps. The first to open was Mooragh camp, a fenced off section of the Mooragh promenade in Ramsey which opened in May 1940.

As the internees arrived, Manxmen left, in particular the Manx Regiment whose batteries helped defend the ports and airbases of the rest of Britain. Eight ships from the Isle of Man Steam Packet Company were at Dunkirk – *King Orry*, *Fenella* and *Mona's Queen* were all sunk, the latter having the distinction of being the first to arrive to collect troops from the beaches; she sunk on her third trip. And back on Mann another airfield was being built at Andreas, this time as a base for Spitfire fighter planes, and Air Sea Rescue with Lysander and Walrus aircraft. The new aerodrome affected more than just the farmers whose land was requisitioned. Andreas Rectory was used as a mess for RAF officers and St Andrew's church tower reduced by half. At 120 feet high it was a landmark throughout the northern plain, but was unfortunately in the way of aircraft using the new Andreas airfield. It was shortened not merely by demolishing the top, but by removing three quarters of the tower and then rebuilding the more decorated upper portion on the lower base. According to Ramsey Moore, one time chairman of the Manx Museum and National Trust, the stones from the middle section were numbered and stored to be put back at the end of the war but the church wardens accepted a compensatory sum of money instead. The money was used to provide an electric pump for the church organ.

St Andrew's church, Kirk Andreas with its shortened tower. It used to be twice the height

122

Despite all the wartime activity it was still the internment camps which made the most impact on the island. By October 1940 approximately 85% of all aliens of enemy nationality living in Britain were interned in the Isle of Man. The camps were everywhere; Onchan, Peel, a camp for women and children in Port St Mary, and one for married couples at Port Erin. Douglas front became a series of camps centred around hotels. The Palace Camp, for example, got its name from its location encompassing Palace Terrace and Palace Road, and consisted of twenty-nine hotels including the Edelweiss, Inglewood, Hydro and Richmond. Other Douglas camps were called the Sefton, Metropole, Granville and Central, and based around hotels of the same name. The Castle Mona shops became the military stores, the Crescent Cinema a depot for camp food and the Falcon Cliff Hotel, now Falcon Cliff Court, became the camps' hospital. 'Mereside', a small hotel in Empire Terrace, was used as Camp HQ. At the time of writing the hotel's history is remembered in the name of its bar and restaurant; HQ Bar.

Some internees were permitted to work on farms or take over certain civilian jobs while Manxmen were away fighting. Although the Manx generally welcomed those detained on the island and were liked and respected in return, some circumstances did cause friction. For example, gas attacks had long been feared throughout Great Britain and civilian respirators were standard issue across the water. Not on Mann however. At first the only people on the island to have masks were the internees who had been issued with them before they arrived. There was also general concern that internees should not receive more food than the civilians outside the wire. Partly to stem British questions on the matter and partly to counter allegations made in a broadcast in English on German radio, Osbert Peake, the Under-Secretary of State for the Home Department in Westminster, on 25 February 1941 issued an official statement about the daily rations and diet of internees on the Isle of Man. According to his statement internees were provided with per week, among other foodstuffs, 2oz of tea, just over 6lbs of bread, 14oz of jam, 4oz of meat on five days but no butter, bacon or eggs. Kosher meat was provided when possible and internees who declined non-kosher meat could be offered fish, lentils, cheese or rice when available instead. By contrast civilians received per week the same amount of tea, less jam (1lb every two months was usual), and often had to manage on roughly half of the meat given to internees, including the 4oz per week bacon ration. On the other hand, bread outside the camps was not rationed, and civilians were entitled to 2oz of butter and 1 egg per week.

Internees were generally separated into different nationalities to reduce the possibility of sectarian violence. One of the internees who had a great effect on Mann was German archaeologist Gerhard Bersu. Jewish ancestry meant that he'd left Germany and was working in Britain when war was declared. He and his wife spent the war in the camp for married couples in Port Erin. At least they slept in the camp. For most of the war Bersu, assisted by his wife and a motley group of volunteers, trundled round the Isle of Man happily excavating prehistoric and Viking remains, including the ship burial at Balladoole (see chapter 3). Rumour has it that so little interest did Bersu and his team have in leaving the island that the armed guard was often roped in to help the excavation work, stashing their rifles in handy hedges until the time came to escort their prisoners back to their camp. Much of the island's knowledge of its past, and the preservation of its prehistoric remains is thanks to the expert German professor and his wartime dedication. A.M. Cubbon, former Director of the Manx Museum and National Trust says in *100 Years of Heritage*: 'representatives of the Manx Museum visit[ed] the site to inspect progress, and surreptitiously dropp[ed] little tins of his beloved snuff into the wellington boots of Gerhard Bersu.' A very small price to pay for such expert help!

Post-war problems – and opportunities

The desire of the Manx to run their own affairs had not gone away and, just as after the First World War more independence was granted to Tynwald, so more was expected after the Second. In 1940, India, for example, had been promised independence in return for their help during the war, and gained it in 1947. The Manx wanted nothing less. Samuel Norris, Member of the House of Keys for North Douglas, had kept the question alive by, in 1942, proposing power-sharing with the Lieutenant Governor in the form of a Manx Cabinet. With the Japanese invading Burma, Field Marshal Rommel launching a new offensive against the British 'Desert Rats' which included the Manx Regiment, and the beginning of the Holocaust, Norris's timing was inauspicious and the matter was shelved until after the war.

In 1946, after general elections in both Mann and the United Kingdom, the time was right for change. An Executive Council was created made up of the five chairmen of the main governmental boards (see chapter 7) – analogous to government ministers in the UK – plus two further members of Tynwald voted to the post by their peers. All appointments were to be

considered by the House of Keys, the Legislative Council and the Lieutenant Governor. The Executive Board was to act as a Manx 'Cabinet' and assist the Lieutenant Governor, who was to be in effect the island's Chancellor of the Exchequer, to govern the island.

Even before the war ended the British monarchy acknowledged the island's part in the defence of the realm by

Fleece drying on fuchsia bushes near Crebbin's Cottage, Cregneash

making it the destination of the first royal visit outside the UK since the war began. Victory in Europe (V later VE) day was 8 May 1945, Victory in Japan (VJ) day was 14 August that same year. Between the two on 4 July 1945 King George VI and Queen Elizabeth arrived by boat for a three-day visit. The following day the king became the first monarch to preside at Tynwald and take the Lord of Man's place on Tynwald Hill.

After the war the Manx people struggled to get the island back to welcoming holiday makers. Only those internees who wanted to stay remained on the island, camps were dismantled and hotel owners repossessed their hotels. After the overcrowding, trauma and damage of wartime, properties were at best extremely shabby and at worst badly damaged with neither the internees nor the military respecting the private properties they had inhabited. The war had exhausted all stocks of raw materials and even simple things like paint were extremely scarce. Food rationing was also still in force. Nevertheless hoteliers smartened up their properties and, in 1946 welcomed a huge number of visitors eager to take their first real holiday for seven years.

For more than seventy years the island had grown as a popular tourist destination and, partly due to a wish to provide the Manx with information about their own history, and partly

A Brief History of the Isle of Man

to provide attractions for tourists, Governor Loch prompted the foundation of the Manx Museum. In 1866 the Manx Museum and Ancient Monument Trustees was founded. It grew steadily in importance and, by the middle of the twentieth century Manx heritage and culture was rightly celebrated. Probably the leading authority on Manx antiquities for much of that time was Philip (P.M.C.) Kermode skilled archaeologist and author of the definitive book on Manx crosses. It was Kermode who discovered that the Manx crosses carry some of the earliest known illustrations of scenes from the Icelandic sagas. So important was his discovery that the Government of Iceland made him a Knight (*Riddari*) of the Order of the Falcon (*Hin íslenzka fálkaorða*). The news of the high honour arrived on 5 September 1932. He was seventy seven. It was the day he died.

Manx heritage was at last being given the recognition it deserved and several important sites were saved from demolition or destruction. In 1938, local builder E.C. Kneale obtained a fifteen-year lease on the Lady Isabella, derelict since the mine closed in 1929, restored it and finally purchased it in 1946. In 1935 the Peggy (see chapter 7) was discovered in Castletown; it became the centre of the Nautical Museum in 1951, while in 1950 the Castletown Town Commissioners gave the grammar school, built in the mid-thirteenth century as a chapel, to the Manx Museum. The National Trust in the UK had been going since 1895, and the Calf of Mann was given into its care in 1937. In 1951 the Manx National Trust was created and soon obtained a long lease on the Calf from its older peer.

The Cregneash Village Folk Museum had its roots, almost literally, in a relatively isolated upland crofting village (*claghan*) containing the last native Manx speakers. The Manx language society (*Yn Cheshaght Ghailechagh*) had been founded in 1899 and was dedicated to preserving and promoting Manx Gaelic. Harry Kelly who died in 1935, lived in Cregneash and was the last person known to speak only Manx. His cottage was donated to the Manx Museum by members of his family and, in 1938, it was the first building to be opened to the

Looking towards the Calf of Man from the Turner's Shed, Cregneash

public (see picture on page 87) in what was to be one of the earliest living museums in Britain. In addition, just after the war and during the 1950s, the Manx Museum, at first with the help of the Irish Folklore Commission, recorded the reminiscences and Manx speech of as many of the older generation of islanders as they could. The museum also corresponded with the descendents of Manx ex-pats to learn the oral history which helps make up the story of Mann.

Sliding into recession...

For over one hundred years the Manx had catered for the huge numbers of visitors who came to spend their holidays on their island. The TT had resumed in 1947 after the hiatus of wartime and continued to draw thousands to the island but some attractions, such as the Marine Drive tramway (see chapter 7) had not re-opened after the war, and others such as the Douglas Head Theatre saw slumps in patronage. In addition the 1950s saw holidays in Spain begin to grow in popularity. Not only were they cheaper and could guarantee good weather, the newly-built hotels were often fitted out to a higher standard. Jugs/basins and a bathroom at the end of the corridor in Victorian hotels in Douglas could not compete with en-suite facilities in new hotels in Spain. Visitor numbers began to decline.

An additional problem was that the holiday season was just that – seasonal. Finding employment for the winter months was a real problem on the Isle of Man and, as holiday makers began to drift elsewhere for their holidays, year-round unemployment became an additional concern. Emigration, the island's barometer of social stability, once again began to increase with around 7,000 mostly young people leaving Mann during the 1950s, around 11% of the population. The problem was exacerbated by the galloping inflation of the 1970s.

Several schemes which would be unthinkable now, were actively proposed to try and improve the island's finances. Although the Isle of Man has no oil of its own, Tynwald was in favour of constructing an oil refinery on the Ayres to process oil shipped from the Middle East on behalf of an American company; a rare and fragile ecosystem would have been lost. The Gaiety Theatre, one of the best surviving Victorian theatres, was planned for demolition and replacement with a shopping mall, flats and offices. Other schemes such as the demolition of Derby Castle and Fort Anne, the sale and dispersal of the contents of the Nunnery estate, and the sale of Bishopscourt were allowed to go ahead.

The Gaiety Theatre. One of the best preserved Victorian theatres in the British Isles

Notwithstanding the island's financial concerns, the Manx people still wanted independence from their UK overlords. Small steps had been taken to secure greater independence but until the 1970s the outward signs of the dominance of the UK – the stamps and coinage – still existed. The Manx government had been printing their own banknotes since 1961, but the island's coinage remained firmly that of the UK. That changed with the introduction of decimalisation in 1971. For the first time for around 130 years the Isle of Man was to have its own coinage.

The first stamp with a Manx identity had been issued in 1958, but was issued by the UK post office. At this time the post office also ran the fledgling – and loss-making(!) – telephone service. Tynwald accepted the principal of an independent Manx post office, but in increasingly difficult times was reluctant also to take on telecommunications. In the seventeenth century John Murray had led the way with coinage by privately producing 'Murray's pence (see chapter 6). Two centuries later in the spring of 1971 Gordon

Above: 1958 stamp, the first to be issued with a Manx identity.
Right: One of the first stamps issued in 1973 by the independent Manx post office. Illustrations for the stamps were painted by Manx artist John Nicholson. This one is of Port St Mary

Quirk followed suit by providing a temporary Post Manninagh during a postal strike by UK postal workers. For stamps he used the paper covers from souvenir matchbox covers which he had been printing in advance of the tourist season, and cancellation franks were provided by a numbering machine previously used for invoices. Later that same year Tynwald began negotiating a Manx take-over of postal services. Not only was the government aiming to emphasise the island's separate identity, it also saw the production of Isle of Man stamps as a way to raise money with stamp collectors around the world. The Manx Post Office came into being on Tynwald day (5 July) 1973.

...and climbing out again

Improving the island's finances became increasingly imperative as the numbers of holidaymakers dwindled. Light industries were encouraged, and investment in hydro electricity reduced the island's dependence on foreign oil. More recently the island has become popular as a film location, and as a supplier of organic produce to the UK market, as well as having an increasing involvement in aerospace technology; it is home to a cluster of space-industry companies, and is fifth in the race to return to the Moon, after China, the US, Russia and India.

Although only 6% of Mann's income now stems from tourism, it is still considered important to the Manx economy. The major annual tourist event is of course the TT races, but from the 1960s onward, facilities have been improved, partly to increase visitor numbers, partly to vary the experience on offer and partly to lengthen the season which the island's location and weather tends to make short. Summerland, opened in 1971 on the old Derby Castle site, was designed to provide artificially sunny conditions year round in the hope of attracting holidaymakers defecting to Spain. Summerland's design and construction was at best frankly experimental and two years later it was destroyed in the one of the worst peacetime fires in twentieth century Britain. Today holidaymakers are much more likely to come to Mann for the scenery, walking, numerous golf courses, to ride on the heritage transport, visit the unique heritage sites or to view rare marine life such as the basking sharks.

Mann is also one of the few places in Britain to offer American-style casino facilities. First proposed in 1956, a casino was approved in 1961 and opened in 1963 in the Castle Mona hotel. It closed temporarily in 1965 as the American syndicate which operated it was accused of financial irregularity. Rebuilt, it moved to a new venue next door and was opened in 1966 by 'James Bond' or rather the actor who played him, Sean Connery. Today the island is a major player in the online gaming market as part of its strategy of encouraging e-business.

Lichen Heath on The Ayres. It is an internationally rare and extremely fragile ecosystem

The principal means by which Tynwald has boosted the Isle of Man's income however was to market it as an off-shore financial centre. The island had long been known as a place of financial advantage and for centuries was often the refuge of UK debtors who knew that their creditors could not legally enforce recovery from debtors across the water. Financial manoeuvrability was after all one of the reasons the Dumbell family came to the island (see chapter 7). History may have repeated itself in 1982 and 1983 when the Isle of Man's Savings and Investment Bank, Investors Mercantile Ltd and Chancellor Finance all collapsed, but new legislation to supervise and control financiers, while still offering them better tax breaks than in the UK, has made the island attractive to financiers. By the early 1980s a quarter of the Manx national income came from the financial sector; today the figure is closer to 40%.

The Isle of Man is not independent of British rule, but nearly so. It is a Crown Dependency, which means that it is neither part of the United Kingdom nor of Great Britain but is a British Island (a political entity into which the Channel Islands fall) and part of the British Isles, which is a geographical term referring to the islands off the north west coast of Europe. The Isle of Man is self governing, but its legislation requires royal assent to become law; since 1981 the Lieutenant Governor, as the Queen's representative, has been permitted to grant royal assent on her behalf. As royal assent has not been refused since 1707 it is deemed to be largely automatic.

Statue of Joey Dunlop overlooking the TT course at Bungalow. A good bike rider and a kind man, he won a record 26 races at TT meetings before being killed in 2000 racing in Estonia. The 26th milestone on the TT course was renamed 'Joey's' in his honour

Tynwald, the Manx parliament, is divided into two chambers, the House of Keys and the Legislative Council. The two chambers are roughly equivalent to the Houses of Commons and Lords in the Westminster parliament, although they do not have precisely the same executive function. Together the Keys and the Legislative Council form the Tynwald Court which authorises and manages island expenditure. The Council of Ministers, formerly the Executive Council, is similar to the Cabinet in the Westminster government, although again does not have a precisely similar function. Previously known as Chairmen of Boards, since 1986 the council's members have assumed the title of Ministers.

Foreseeing the Future

From being batted about between warring neighbours the Isle of Man has emerged as a small independent country fiercely proud of its language, heritage and traditions. Much less reliant on the sea for communication, food and trade, its island status still quarantines Mann from developments in which it wishes to take no part. The foot and mouth crises which hit the UK in 2001, for example, did not spread to the Isle of Man. The Manx took great care to protect their island from infection, even going to the lengths of cancelling that year's TT. Neither does the Isle of Man have a particular problem with illegal immigration. The island's population is certainly fluid. Foreign nationals come to the island to work, and young people leave to study and work overseas, but many return later in life, and those who don't usually maintain close contact with their roots. Such has been the Manx way for hundreds of years. No-one has a crystal ball, but one or two predictions may be attempted – and probably with the usual inaccurate results.

The Isle of Man is not a member of the European Union (EU) but has what is euphemistically called a 'special relationship' stemming from when Britain joined the Common Market in 1972; Westminster negotiated an associate membership in the Economic Community for its Crown Dependencies. It seems unlikely that Mann will seek membership of the EU in its own right while its special relationship means that it can create wealth through offshore finance but still enjoy unrestricted trade with EU members. On the other hand the EU could make life difficult for offshore financial centres, possibly by re-erecting customs barriers and preventing free trade. Manx income from finance probably means that it would not relinquish its offshore finance status but would therefore have to market its goods beyond the European Economic Area or pay punishing taxation.

Providing that trade barriers were not erected against it, the Isle of Man would probably join the Eurozone were the UK to do so. The island briefly considered adopting the American dollar (in 1974 to try to stem galloping inflation caused by oil prices) but Tynwald has already passed the necessary legislation should a move to the Euro be deemed attractive.

At the beginning of the twenty-first century global warming is of global concern. Depending on which research is accepted, the British Isles are either going to become much colder or much warmer. One of the predictions made is that global warming could disrupt the warm waters of the Gulf Stream which would result in the temperature dropping around five degrees in the latitude of the Irish Sea. The islands would have much in common with Greenland today. Mann's farming community would be badly hit, but with its impressive range of hills the island might turn itself into a ski resort.

Generally warmer world temperatures are already causing ice caps to melt and seas to rise. 15,000 years ago glacial deposits left by the last ice age formed the northern end of Mann (see chapter 1). At the same time melting ice caused by a warmer climate caused the seas to rise and turn Mann into an island. Fifteen millennia later, rising sea water might again shape the land, reclaiming much of the northern plain, turning what is left into a salt marsh and returning Mann to much the same shape it had in 13,000BC. The wheel of time turns and those living on the island will be ready for whatever is turned up. As the Manx say: *myr shegin dy ve, bee eh*; what must be, will be.

CHAPTER 9

SELECTED MYTHS & MYSTERIES; THE ALTERNATIVE HISTORY

If you stand on the summit of Snaefell on a clear day you can see seven kingdoms, or so the story goes: Mann (of course), England, Wales, Scotland, Ireland, the ocean, which is Neptune's Kingdom and heaven, the Kingdom of God. From Snaefell you can see the great panorama of neighbouring islands circling around Mann in the centre, like the rim of a tea cup circling the bubbles in the middle. If the light is right – and it doesn't happen often – the islands of Britain seem close enough for you to reach out your hand and pluck Scafell Pike from the Lake District or cradle the Mountains of Mourne in the palm of your hand.

From the Mountains of Mourne it naturally appears possible to cradle the Isle of Man in your palm, and an Irish giant once did just that. Fionn mac Cumhaill (Finn MacCooil) had fallen out with his neighbour giant in Scotland. During the ensuing fight the anonymous Scottish giant fled Ireland by way of the giant's causeway. Enraged at his escape Fionn scooped up a handful of earth to hurl at his retreating back but his throw fell short. A giant's handful is a lot of earth and, when it landed in the middle of the Irish Sea, it created the Isle of Man. The hole left in Ireland filled with water and became Lough Neagh, the third largest lake in Europe.

Fionn mac Cumhaill is also responsible for the Isle of Man's own 'atlantis' story. The inhabitants of a small island off the east coast of Mann were once unwise enough to insult Fionn. Angered, the giant turned them to stone, sinking their island to the bottom of the sea. Every seven years it rises out of the sea near Port Soderick or perhaps near Bulgham, the location varies, and the inhabitants are reanimated. Oddly enough, islands do occasionally appear off the east coast of Mann, but they're considered to be either the land across, or mirages of the Welsh coast. Maybe.

The Calf of Man. The small island between the Calf and the mainland is called Kitterland. Calf Sound and Little Sound run either side of it

Fionn appears to have had a lot to do with shaping the island he inadvertently created. He lived on it for a while, until exception was taken to his presence by a buggane, a supernatural creature often intent on evil. The buggane tried to drive Fionn away and the two held a great battle at Rushen. Up until then the Calf of Man had been part of the Manx mainland, but Fionn's feet wore away the ground as he took his stand against the buggane and carved out Calf Sound and Little Sound on either side of Kitterland. The buggane meanwhile was standing between Bradda Mooar and

Mull Hill. During the struggle his feet wore away the rock to create Port Erin Bay. This time it was Fionn who gave way, the buggane pulling out one of his own teeth to fling it after the fleeing giant. The tooth bounced off Fionn's back and landed in the sea where it turned into the Chicken Rock. Partly because it stemmed from a buggane, and partly because Fionn cursed it when running away, the rock has been a hazard to sailors ever since.

Fionn mac Cumhaill might be credited with creating the Isle of Man, but it's another figure of legend who gave the island its name. According to mediaeval texts Mannin McLir was a celebrated merchant and sea pilot who lived on the island and was skilled at reading the weather. Over the years Mannin became confused with Manannan, the Celtic equivalent of Neptune

and McLir transmogrified into Mac y Leir or son of the sea. As Manannan he's credited with being the island's first ruler and after whom Mann is supposed to have been named.

Legend says that Manannan protected his kingdom by enveloping it in mist so that enemies couldn't find it and invade. Even today, low cloud is often referred to as the cloak of Manannan. The marram grass spread on the processional way each

Manannan's Cloak over Agneash

Tynwald Day (see appendix 3) is a traditional tribute to Mann's traditional protector. Often referred to as rushes, tradition is also a factor in their provenance. They were supplied by Ballaleece Farm, about half a mile west of St John's along the current A1, and their production for use on Tynwald Day was a condition of the farm's tenancy.

Manannan is also responsible for the origin of the three legs of Mann. According to one version of the legend the sea god turned himself into a three-legged fiery hoop which rolled down from North Barrule to rout Manx invaders. Another legend claims the triskelion to be the result of what we should now

A modern flying saucer! Actually a radar station on Cronk ny Arrey near Cregneash

recognise as a visit by a flying saucer. Back in the time of the Druids a group of fishermen was driven ashore by a storm and set up camp on an unspecified Manx beach. As they were huddled around their fire, a huge fiery wheel supported on three armoured legs emerged from the stormclouds, hovered above them partially obscured by mist, and then floated up the cliff and inland. The seaman took the apparition to be an omen of their escape and the three mailed legs became a lucky symbol thereafter.

Perhaps it is fitting that a god gives his name to a large island, and a man gives his name to a tiny one. Baron Kitter supposedly lived in Mann around eight hundred years ago. His castle was on the top of South Barrule and he loved hunting the great deer and purrs or wild pig which roamed the Isle of Man then. He also hunted on the Calf, which was rumoured to be the home of a fabulous red deer. While he was away his castle caught fire and his cook shouted loudly for help. Hearing the cries and seeing the fire Baron Kitter set off immediately to cross the Sound. Reckless in his haste the

Rocks and sea near Poyllvaaish

baron sailed carelessly and his boat struck a rock about half-way across. Most of his men were drowned as his boat sank, but the baron was thrown onto the rock. Unable to cross either to the Manx mainland or to the Calf the baron clung to the rock until he died. It has been called Kitterland ever since.

Christianity arrives, as do the Vikings

By tradition the first people to arrive on Mann landed at what is now Castletown, although their landing was hotly disputed by the little people or fairies who lived on the island. Gradually the human invaders won the day, possessing first the land in Rushen and gradually extending their rule over the whole island. Not that the fairies, or as the Manx say 'themselves', left the island of course, but they took care to hide from view.

Also near Castletown is the site of a tradition which appears to have been going on an incredibly long time. About two hundred years ago a Periwinkle Fair was held annually on Shrove Tuesday near the shore at Poyllvaaish, principally for the sale of periwinkles and gingerbread. During Lent it was usual for people to abstain from eating meat – most couldn't afford to eat much anyway – and the Periwinkle Fair was therefore ideally timed to usher in the eating of fish and shellfish. Excavations at nearby Balladoole have revealed a midden containing a huge number of periwinkle shells. The midden was dated as stemming from before the Bronze Age so it appears that Periwinkle Fair had its foundations in a tradition dating back more than three thousand years.

St Patrick himself crossed from Ireland to bring Christianity to Mann, or so the story goes; St Patrick's Isle was named in his honour. Great saints perform great miracles and he was supposed to have crossed on horseback. He was also in something of a hurry as he was being chased by a sea monster. Taking a great leap to avoid the monster the horse landed on Corrin's Hill. The sea beast crashed into the cliff below, turning into stone as it did so. It's still there, *Carrick yn Ardnieu*, the rock of the serpent. As both horse and rider were thirsty after their hasty passage, a spring gushed out of the rock where the horse's feet had landed and the saint and his mount were able to drink. The spring became known as the Holy Well of St Patrick, or occasionally as Chibbyr Sheeant (Blessed Well) or Chibbr yn Argid (Well of the Silver). The first Christians on the island were baptised in the well by the saint. The spring was also reputed to have healing properties, particularly for eyes, and modern analysis has found some basis for the claim. The water contains silver compounds and silver is noted for being able to purify water.

St Maughold being converted and baptised by St Patrick, Jurby church.

Like many visitors to Mann, St Patrick had a look round while he was on the island and visited a keeill on Ballafreer Farm not far from Colby Glen. Immediately renamed Keeill Pheric (St Patrick's church) in honour of the saint's visit, it also gave its name to Ballakilpheric. It's said that the saint trod on a thorn while on his way to the keeill and cursed the land on which the thorn had grown saying that it would never bear a crop. Apparently it never has.

Whether St Patrick really came to the Isle of Man in person is unclear, but one of his disciples arrived, although in a rather unusual way. St Maughold started life as a thief and murderer living in Ulster, where he decided to expose St Patrick as a fraud, failed and was converted. The new penitent begged punishment for his previous wickedness and so was cast adrift in a small coracle, with his feet shackled together (ferry companies take note). Drifting with the tide he eventually landed on Mann. St Maughold's Well or Chibbyr Vaghal marks where he came ashore and gave thanks for his deliverance. The key to his

St Maughold's Well or Chibbyr Vaghal marking where St Maughold came ashore. Just behind the photographer is an almost sheer drop to the sea!

shackles was found in the belly of a fish and, strengthened by this miracle, St Maughold began his holy work on the island, finally becoming its first Bishop around AD500.

The Vikings arrived in the latter part of the eighth century, and some of the most enduring Manx myths arose around Norseman Godred Crovan. In Manx Godred becomes Goree, and King Godred Crovan is therefore King Gorree, or King Orry. When he landed in Lhen in

A Brief History of the Isle of Man

1079, it was a brilliant star-lit night. Those who gathered to see who he was asked where he had come from and he pointed upwards to the Milky Way, saying that it led to his home. Ever since then the Milky Way has been known as *Raad Mooar Ree Goree*, or the Great Way of King Orry. His grave, the chambered cairn Gretch Veg, is said to be in the largest Neolithic monument on Mann. Sky Hill, where the battle which eventually gave him the island was fought (see chapter 3), is also supposed to be the venue of a large fairy city.

One hundred and fifty years after King Orry – Godred Crovan – his namesake Godred II was King of Mann and the Isles. His brother-in-law, Somerled, sought to oust Godred from the throne and landed at Ramsey in 1158. Afraid lest their meagre possessions be plundered locals stacked valuables in Maughold Church, and placed their livestock in the churchyard, trusting to the great saint to protect them and theirs from harm. While Somerled and Godred jockeyed for position Gilcolm, one of Somerled's generals, wanted to break into Maughold church, steal anything valuable and take the animals to feed his army. Somerled refused, saying that if he did so, he acted on his own responsibility and must take the consequences. And consequences there were.

King Orry's Grave near Laxey. Supposed to be the last resting place of Godred Croven it is a stone age burial mound

The attack was planned for first light and the Maughold people spent the night in prayer and lamentation, pleading for the saint's aid. Answering their pleas St Maughold appeared to Gilcolm in a dream, dressed in white and holding a shepherd's staff. The saint then stabbed Gilcolm three times in the chest with his staff. He lived just long enough to tell what had happened. In terror at the saint's retribution, Gilcolm's men fled the island.

The invisible world

The Christian church considered itself to be constantly fighting an invisible battle between the belief in fairies on the one hand, and the fairies themselves on the other. Kirk Malew has an extremely rare pre-reformation paten – the plate from which the bread of holy communion is served – and stories tell that its communion cup is of even stranger provenance. A traveller had been lured by strange music to a place where the little people were feasting. Among them he saw the likenesses of former neighbours who had disappeared in mysterious circumstances. One warned him not to eat or drink anything as he would then be, like his former friends, unable to return home. The traveller was provided with a silver cup filled with sweet-smelling drink, but, despite his raging thirst, he resisting tasting it. Throwing it onto the ground, the fairies rose in dismay and disappeared, leaving him with the cup. Returning home he asked his vicar what he should do with it as he was frightened of its possible power. The vicar, either through piety or greed, suggested that it could have no power if devoted to the service of the church so the traveller gave the cup to him. Malew Parish Church certainly once possessed

Maughold Church and churchyard looking south west. The tall monument in the centre is to Hall Caine and is designed by Archibald Knox

a communion cup dating from around 1781 but as it was one of a pair, both of which were engraved with a shield of arms neither is likely to be of fairy provenance. Pity.

As fairies have been thought to inhabit the area around Castletown since before there were men on Mann it's little wonder that the foundations of Castle Rushen were built by themselves. The castle has long had the reputation for having numerous subterranean tunnels and chambers, making it larger below ground than it is above. Many unsuccessful attempts have been made to explore the passages with explorers returning out of their senses or not returning at all. The lowest dungeons of the castle were of course closed against the prying eyes of men as they were inhabited by giants. Some say they are still.

Fairies seem to make good construction workers and a number of Manx builders appear to have had supernatural help. The Tholt-y-Will landowner wanted to build a large house below Snaefell and employed men to quarry the requisite stones from the beach. The quarried material included one large white block which he intended to use as a hearth stone. Too large to move with the muscle power available, the team knocked off for the night. On the following day they gathered more men to heave the stones up from the beach. When the crowd assembled they found that a phynnodderee, a Manx creature, half man, half beast and with prodigious strength, had been before them and moved the two hundred tons of stone to the building site in a single night. Grateful to the phynnodderee the gentleman built his house. The huge white block was unsuitable for a hearth stone so it was used elsewhere, but can still, apparently, be seen.

Greeba must have been an area well known for supernatural happenings. The Curragh Glass or marshy pool situated in the valley below Greeba Mountain was supposed to be a favourite place for testing for witchcraft. If the unfortunate woman did not suffocate in the marsh she was guilty of being a witch and rolled from the top of Slieau Whuallian in a barrel filled with

A Brief History of the Isle of Man

spikes. Although there is a famous inscription on the Smelt monument in Castletown about the column also marking the site where witches were executed, almost nobody in the Isle of Man was put to death for witchcraft, probably because so many Manx people believed in them and used their services.

Greeba is also the site of a more famous supernatural happening.

Kirk Malew, not far from Castletown. Confusingly the dedication could be to either St Lua or St Lupus

Depending on which version you believe, the church of St Trinian at the foot of Greeba Mountain was built either by monks or by a sailor grateful for being saved from a hurricane. Either way, the buggane who lived on the mountain didn't like the idea of being woken up by church bells ringing at all hours so came and tore the roof off the church; he knew that people wouldn't use it if it weren't finished. Every time the roof was completed the buggane would come down the mountain and tear it off again. Timothy, a poor tailor, trying to earn a little extra money, wagered that the next time the roof was completed he would spend the night in the church making a pair of breeches.

Arriving at dusk he began work. He cut and sewed as fast as he could as the breeches had to be completed or he wouldn't win his wager. All the time he kept a sharp eye open for the buggane. Towards midnight the head of the buggane rose out of the beaten earth of the church floor. Faster and faster sewed the tailor and higher and higher rose the buggane. Just as the monster pulled himself out of the ground the tailor put in the last stitch. Scooping up his sewing kit Timothy ran from the church as the buggane ripped off the roof and gave chase. Knowing that his pursuer could not enter consecrated ground Timothy fled to St Runius's Church, now known as Marown Old Church, and hid in the churchyard. So incensed was the buggane that it tore off its own head and threw it after the tailor. It missed but hit the ground and exploded presumably destroying the buggane. Nevertheless no-one wanted to tempt fate by replacing the roof on St Trinian's and it has remained unfinished since the seventeenth century. The tailor's scissors and the key to St Trinian's church used to be displayed at the Highlander Inn nearby.

St Trinian's church near Greeba. Still roofless, after 300 years

Saltwater...and blood

During the time of Oliver Cromwell fewer ships visited the Isle of Man and the lack of sea traffic gave merpeople the opportunity of visiting the Manx shore uninterrupted. The Manx call them simply *ben varrey* and *dooiney varrey*; women of the sea and men of the sea. For hundreds of years the herring catch was extremely important to the Manx economy. Even today the oath sworn by the Deemsters is that they will 'without respect or favour or friendship, love or gain, consanguinity or affinity, envy or malice, execute the laws of this isle justly between our Sovereign Lord the King and his subjects within this isle, and betwixt party and party, as indifferently as the herring's backbone doth lie in the midst of the fish.' The protective mist which hides the island from its enemies may be attributed to the care of Manannan, but the mist which arises to confuse the seafarer and make the trader miss the Manx ports is thought to be the work of offended mermaids and mermen.

Sailors are notoriously superstitious and were concerned to propitiate whatever fates there were in order to get a good catch. Up until the end of the nineteenth century fishermen would light a fire of dry heather inside their boat, touching every part of the boat with the burning fronds to exorcise evil spirits. In similar vein, no Peel

Bulgham Bay from an MER trailer. The rising mist means that the merfolk are angry

fishing boat would leave the harbour third in the fleet, so the third and fourth boats out often roped themselves together temporarily to count as one.

Many countries have a belief in the magical properties of blood, particularly that of a leader. When Charles I of England was executed on 30 January 1649 the scaffold and floor were covered with black cloth. This might have added to the spectacle (and, in a practical sense made the cleaning up easier) but it also provided a large number of saleable souvenirs. After the beheading the executioner sold pieces of cloth soaked in the king's blood to the crowd. A similar scene occurred at the execution of William Christian, aka Illiam Dhone, by firing squad on 2 January 1663 (see chapter 6). According to tradition, blankets were spread where Christian stood so that his blood did not fall onto the ground. No records appear to exist about what was done with them but, presuming they were used to wrap the body, one or more might well have been kept by his supporters. Even if the English garrison was formally instructed to destroy them, there is such a thing as bribery...

Calendar customs

Every year on 5 July, old midsummer's day, Manx dignitaries meet on Tynwald Hill, St John's to proclaim new laws. The laws are read in English and in Manx and, until so read, are not binding (see chapter 8 and appendix 3). Nowadays the titles and abstracts are all that's read as legislation has grown more complicated. St John's is in the parish of German so islanders say that the laws have to be read in Manx, in English and in German.

The Tynwald ceremony stretches back more than one thousand years and marks the

A Brief History of the Isle of Man

world's oldest parliament, but its timing owes much to Scandinavian legend. For people living within the Arctic circle who experience twenty-four hours of darkness during the winter, midsummer had special significance. Midsummer celebrations were and are very important to the Scandinavian people. According to Norse mythology Baldr was the son of Odin and Frigg, famed for his goodness, peace and joy, and associated with the beneficial effects of the sun. His life culminated at midsummer, during which fires were lit to prefigured Baldr's funeral pyre and hoops of fire were rolled down the hillside to symbolise the sun's decline – we're back to the origins of the three legs of Mann again (see above). As was usual, the Christian church, unable to stop such pagan celebrations, adopted them and used them for its own ends. St John ousted Baldr and the midsummer celebrations became officially in his honour. In some stories, sacred wells appeared from the hoofprints of Baldr's horse and there is a Manx saying: *Lane croie cabbyl dy ushtey L'aal Eoin feeu mayl Vannin*, or 'a full horseshoe of water on John's feast day is worth the rent of Mann'.

Not only is St John's church integral to the Tynwald ceremonies (see appendix 3) but every Tynwald participant also wears a buttonhole of *Bollan-feaill-Eoin* (literally the wort of the vigil of John) or mugwort. Sometimes called bollan bane it is not the same as St John's Wort which does not grow naturally on Mann. Traditionally worn in the hat or on the head, mugwort protects against supernatural harm. By Scandinavian custom, wearers of bollan bane are also demonstrating loyalty to their monarch.

Mann has often been supremely indifferent to the changes in the calendar and has continued to celebrate various festivals as they fell in the old-style calendar, long after such festivals were moved to fit with the new calendar elsewhere – Tynwald is a good example. As late as the beginning of the nineteenth century many Manx considered that the first day of the year and the official beginning of winter fell on 12 November. Called *Oie houney* in Manx, it's the equivalent of Hallowe'en. On this day people let land, paid rent and hired men servants for the coming year. They also thought that the weather on 12 November gave a good indication of what could be expected in the year to come. Six months later, on 12 May, it was traditional for houses to be let, the half-year rent to be paid, and animals to be set aside for fattening over the summer. It was also the turn of the women servants to take up their new places.

Fairy Bridge on the A5. Don't forget to wave to Themselves as you cross

Servants who wished to leave their masters' employment were required to give notice on particular days. Sometimes the master was absent on such days, either through business or because he didn't want to accept a particular servant's resignation. In those circumstances custom allowed the servant to go to the master's chair, or the door to his master's room and make a nick in the wood. Providing the servant had witnesses to his actions, the nick was considered tantamount to a letter of resignation. Perhaps a multi-nicked chair was the sign of a poor master.

There were also interesting differences in customs between the north and south of Mann, as divided along the ridge of hills which forms the island's backbone. 6 December, *Laa'l Catreeney* or St Catherine's Day (old style), in the south side of the island is when land is transferred from one occupier to another as different fields and farms change hands. On the north side of Mann the same thing occurs on 11 December, *Laa'l Andreays* or St Andrew's Day.

The north-south divide is also noticeable in the traditional division between the rights of women in the north and the south. The Isle of Man, despite its name, has usually been ahead of its time when it comes to the rights of women. Not only was it the first place in the world to give women the vote (see chapter 7), women could also make their own will even if their husbands were alive; across the water husbands were the sole owners of what nowadays would be considered joint property. Women in the south of Mann could dispose of one half of the joint property by will; those in the north only one third. The discrepancy is said to go back to the Battle of Santwat in 1098 when, according to tradition, the southern women fought alongside their men to gain the victory (but see chapter 3). Their additional rights were thought to be their reward.

Modern Myths

The nineteenth and twentieth centuries have also had their share of supernatural interest, much of it created to provide attractions for tourists. Several parishes claim to have a Fairy Bridge, for example; the celebrated bridge over Santon Burn where everyone is exhorted to greet the fairies for fear of bad luck is thought to have been a nineteenth century tourist attraction. Nice though, and I dare say the little people don't mind.

A much later attraction created for the tourist market was the Witches Mill, a twentieth century museum of witchcraft. It was opened in 1951 by Cecil Williamson in a disused windmill which was said, at least by him, to have been the home of the Arbory witches. He also installed a resident witch in the person of Gerald Gardner. The two men eventually fell out and Williamson sold the mill to Gardner who continued to run it as a tourist attraction until around 1973. Williamson moved the museum back to the UK and, after being ousted from

The Witches Mill, Castletown, Isle of Man.   *Photo : E. Nägele, John Hinde Studios.*

The Witches Mill from a postcard, as it looked in the 1960s. It is now residential accommodation

various locations established it at Boscastle in Cornwall in 1960. It still exists.

Today the mill has been converted to residential accommodation. It was unusual, but not because of supernatural happenings. Windmills are extremely rare on Mann, with the sites of less than a dozen known. The island is subject to strong blustery winds, which are unsuitable for milling, but has a good and generally unfailing water supply. Milling on Mann was therefore almost always done by waterwheel.

Recent supernatural tales have less to do with recording the history of the island, and more to do with affecting it. Early myths such as that of Fionn mac Cumhaill, explain the island's creation, later ones such as the Witches Mill draw visitors who bring wealth to the island – a modern development on 'crossing the palm with silver', perhaps. Perhaps a legend cannot really be a legend until it has time on its side. Even so, by supporting the island's tourist industry, the little people continue to influence its history.

Fortune telling

A great witch, or some say a great wizard, who lived many years ago was known for the accuracy of her prophecy. Caillagh-ny-Faashagh (sometimes called Caillagh-ny-Ghueshag) lived in Foxdale but is said to have foretold many events which subsequently came to pass. She prophesied the Battle of Santwat in 1098 and foretold the founding of the mines in Foxdale. She said that the mountains of Mann would be cut over with roads and iron horses would gallop over them to the inn at the top of Snaefell; the iron horses of the Snaefell Mountain Railway, perhaps?

At Port-e-Vullen. Nothing else to say really

In her last prophesies she said that Mann and Scotland will come so close that a Scotswoman and a Manxwoman would be able to fold washing across the gap. Sand and shingle is indeed building up on the Point of Ayre, although there's a long way to go before it meets Scotland. Caillagh-ny-Faashagh also said that the rulers of Mann will be compelled to flee. The prophesy hasn't yet come true, but *traa dy-liooar* there's time enough…

APPENDIX 1   KINGS AND THINGS

Almost any community or group of people will have a leader, whether formalised or not. Kings and, later, Pharaohs had ruled Ancient Egypt from as early as 3,000 BC, but it was not until the late Bronze Age, and the development of a perceived need to defend settled homesteads, that rulers of lands, rather than tribal leaders, became the norm in most parts of Northern Europe. The following is a list of rulers who believed the Isle of Man to fall under their domain, plus their other holdings and country of origin if applicable. It should be remembered, however, that the Isle of Man was often not considered as a separate identity by the countries which surrounded it, so the idea of formal rule probably didn't exist before the advent of the Vikings, and was often not taken into account after it. As the ruling dynasties of the Scandinavian countries were all interrelated, holdings could pass from, for example, England to Mann to Denmark and back again merely by succession. In addition, the uncertainty of some of the records may mean that dates, particularly the earlier ones, may vary by a year or two. Note: the dates given are the dates of the reign, not the life-span of the ruler.

Dates	Ruler	Country/holdings
445-452	Niall	High King of Ireland
452-463	Lóegaire	High King of Ireland
463-482	Ailill Molt	High King of Ireland
482-507	Lugaid	High King of Ireland
507-534	Muirchertach I	High King of Ireland
534-544	Tuathal Máelgarb	High King of Ireland
544-565	Diarmait I	High King of Ireland
565-566	Forggus	High King of Ireland (co-regent)
	Domnall Ilchelgach	High King of Ireland (co-regent)
566-569	Ainmire	High King of Ireland
569-572	Báetán I	High King of Ireland (co-regent)
	Eochaid	High King of Ireland (co-regent)
572-586	Báetán II	High King of Ireland
586-598	Áed	High King of Ireland
598-604	Áed Sláine	High King of Ireland (co-regent)
	Colmán Rímid	High King of Ireland (co-regent)
604-612	Áed Uaridnach	High King of Ireland
612-615	Máel Cobo	High King of Ireland
615-628	Suibne Menn	High King of Ireland
616-633	Edwin	King of Northumbria (claimed Mann)
628-642	Domnall	High King of Ireland
642-654	Conall Cáel	High King of Ireland (co-regent)
642-658	Cellach	High King of Ireland (co-regent; ruled alone 654-658)
658-665	Diarmait II	High King of Ireland (co-regent)
	Blathmac	High King of Ireland (co-regent)
665-671	Sechnussach	High King of Ireland
671-675	Cennfáelad	High King of Ireland
675-695	Fínsnechta Fledach	High King of Ireland
695-704	Loingsech	High King of Ireland
704-710	Congal Cenmagair	High King of Ireland
710-722	Fergal	High King of Ireland
722-724	Fogartach	High King of Ireland
724-728	Cináed	High King of Ireland
728-734	Flaithbertach	High King of Ireland (deposed)
734-743	Áed Allán	High King of Ireland
743-763	Domnall Midi	High King of Ireland
763-770	Niall Frossach	High King of Ireland
770-797	Donnchad Midi	High King of Ireland
797-800	Áed Oirdnide	High King of Ireland (deposed)

Between 800 and 841 Vikings ruled Mann. They were originally from Norway, but by this time also based in Ireland. The Norwegian monarchy was founded in 841 when Halfdan subjugated his peers and created the first ruling family. The King of Norway often sent a deputy to rule Mann in his stead, with greater or lesser success. Nominally under Norwegian rule, the Isle of Man was actually often under the thumb of whoever had the power to take and hold it.

841-858	Halfdan the Black	King of Norway (abdicated)
858-928	Harald I, 'Fairhair'	King of Norway
928-933	Eirik I, 'Bloodaxe'	King of Norway (deposed)
933-959	Haakon I, 'the Good'	King of Norway
959-974	Harald II, 'Greycloak'	King of Norway
974-994	Earl Haakan Sigurdsson	King of Norway
994-999	Olav I	King of Norway
999-1015	Earl Eirik	King of Norway (abdicated)
1015-1016	Earl Svein	King of Norway (deposed)
1016-1028	St Olav II	King of Norway
1028-1035	Cnut, 'the Great'	King of Denmark, England and Norway
1035-1040	Harold I, 'Harefoot'	King of England (regent 1035-1037)
1040-1042	Harthacnut	King of England
1042-1066	St Edward, 'the Confessor'	King of England
?-1070	Godred, 'son of Sitric'	King of Mann
1070-1079	Fingal	King of Mann
1079-1088	Godred, 'Croven'	King of Mann, Dublin, Leinster and parts of Scotland
1088-1095	Lagman	King of Mann and the Isles
1095-1098	Muirchertach II	High King of Ireland (sent Donald son of Teige to be caretaker King of the Isles. He proved a tyrant and was driven away.)
1098-1103	Magnus III, 'Barelegs'	King of Norway, Mann and the Isles
1103-1153	Olaf I, 'the Dwarf'	King of Mann and the Isles
1153-1154	Reginald plus two brothers	Kings in Mann (co-regents)
1154-1158	Godred II	King of Mann and the Isles (defeated)
1158-1164	Somerled	King of Argyll, Mann and the Isles
1164	Reginald	King of Mann and the Isles (for four days – defeated)
1164-1187	Godred II	King of Mann and the Isles (resumed the throne)
1188-1226	Reginald I	King of Mann and the Isles (defeated)
1226-1237	Olaf II	King of Mann and the Isles
1237-1249	Harald	King of Mann and the Isles (drowned)
1249	Reginald II	King of Mann and the Isles (for 24 days – defeated)
1249-1250	Harald II	King of Mann and the Isles
1250-1252	John	King of Mann and the Isles (claimant)
1252-1265	Magnus IV	King of Mann and the Isles (1263-1265 King of Mann only)
1266-1286	Alexander III	King of Scotland
1286-1290	Margaret	Queen of Scotland (died aged 7)
1290-1307	Edward I	King of England
1307-1313	Edward II	King of England
1313-1316	Robert I 'the Bruce'	King of Scotland
1317-?	Edward II	King of England

Between 1317 and 1329 the Scots and the English both claimed Mann and its rule passed backwards and forwards between them.

?-1329	Robert I 'the Bruce'	King of Scotland
1329-1334	Edward III	King of England

In 1334 the right to rule in Mann was first granted to a member of the English nobility by the English crown. Although holding the title by the grace of the English king of the time, the King of Mann became in fact, if not in law, absolute ruler of the island. Where appropriate members of the nobility are therefore listed as rulers of Mann, rather than the English kings to whom they at least nominally owed allegiance.

1334-1344	William Montacute	King of Mann, 1st Earl of Salisbury

1344-1393	William Montacute	Lord of the Isles of Mann and Wight, 2nd Earl of Salisbury (sold Mann)
1393-1399	William le Scrope	King of Mann, 1st Earl of Wiltshire
1399-1405	Henry Percy	King of Mann, 1st Earl of Northumberland
1405-1414	John Stanley	King of Mann, Knight
1414-1437	John Stanley	King of Mann, Knight
1437-1459	Thomas Stanley	King of Mann, 1st Baron Stanley
1459-1504	Thomas Stanley	King of Mann, 1st Earl of Derby
1504-1521	Thomas Stanley	Lord of Mann, 2nd Earl of Derby
1521-1572	Edward Stanley	Lord of Mann, 3rd Earl of Derby
1572-1593	Henry Stanley	Lord of Mann, 4th Earl of Derby
1593-1594	Ferdinando Stanley	Lord of Mann, 5th Earl of Derby
1594-1603	Elizabeth I	Queen of England, Lord of Mann
1603-1607	James VI and I	King of Scotland and England, Lord of Mann
1607-1608	Henry Howard	Lord of Mann, 1st Earl of Northampton,
1608-1609	Robert Cecil	Lord of Mann, 1st Earl of Salisbury
1610-1642	William Stanley	Lord of Mann, 6th Earl of Derby
[1612-1627	Elizabeth Stanley	Wife of the 6th Earl, largely ruled Mann in her husband's stead.
1627-1642	James Stanley	Son of Elizabeth and the 6th Earl. While still Lord Strange (i.e. before inheriting the earldom) he took over the administration of the island on his mother's death]
1642-1651	James Stanley	Lord of Mann, 7th Earl of Derby
1649-1660	Thomas Fairfax	Lord of Mann (during the Commonwealth and Protectorate; appointed by parliament before the earl's death), 3rd Baron Fairfax
1660-1672	Charles Stanley	Lord of Mann, 8th Earl of Derby
1672-1702	William Stanley	Lord of Mann, 9th Earl of Derby
1702-1736	James Stanley	Lord of Mann, 10th Earl of Derby
1736-1764	James Murray	Lord of Mann, 2nd Duke of Atholl
1764-1765	John Murray	Lord of Mann, 3rd Duke of Atholl (held in right of his wife Charlotte; sold Mann)
1765-1820	George III	King of England, Lord of Mann
1820-1830	George IV	King of England, Lord of Mann
1830-1837	William IV	King of England, Lord of Mann
1837-1901	Victoria	Queen of England, Lord of Mann (note: Victoria preferred to be called Lady of Mann)
1901-1910	Edward VII	King of England, Lord of Mann
1910-1936	George V	King of England, Lord of Mann
1936	Edward VIII	King of England, Lord of Mann (abdicated)
1936-1952	George VI	King of England, Lord of Mann
1952-	Elizabeth II	Queen of England, Lord of Mann

APPENDIX 2   BISHOPS OF SODOR AND MAN

The Bishopric of Sodor and Man was ratified by the papal bull of Pope Anastastius IV in 1154 and was created out of territory traditionally ruled by bishops from York, England and Nidaros (Trondheim), Norway. The merger was not accepted by the archbishops of the old territories who insisted on retaining the right to consecrate bishops of their own choosing. The political tension between Scandinavia, Scotland, England and Ireland also influenced who appointed the bishops and whether they were accepted by all others. As a result Sodor and Man occasionally had two or more bishops. Many of the dates are therefore speculative and a few may overlap.

Dates	Bishop	Notes
c. 1050	Roolwer	
c. 1080	William Hamond	Manxman.
?1138	Wimund	Possibly Bishop of the Isles and not Mann
	Gamaliel	Buried at Peterborough, England
1152-1170	Reginald	Norwegian
c.1158-c.1164	Christinus	From Argyll, Scotland. Died at Ulster, Ireland
c.1164-1203	Michael	Manxman. Died at Fountains Abbey
1203-1217	Nicholas	From Argyll, Scotland. Died at Ulster, Ireland
1217-?	Reginald	Buried in Rushen Abbey
d.1226	John	Died in a fire at Jervaulx, England
1226-1247	Simon	From Argyll, Scotland. Died at the church of St Michael the Archangel. Buried in St German's church, St Patrick's Isle
1247-1249	Laurence	Formerly Archdeacon in Mann. Drowned off Shetland with King Harald
1249-1252	Vacant	
1252-1274	Richard	Died at Langley, Cumbria. Buried Furness Abbey
1274-1303	Mark	From Galloway, Scotland. Buried in St German's church, St Patrick's Isle
1303-1305	Vacant	
1305-1321	Alan	From Galloway, Scotland. Buried Rothesay, Isle of Bute.
1321-1324	Gilbert MacLelan	From Galloway, Scotland. Buried Rothesay, Isle of Bute.
1324-1327	Bernard	Scottish. Buried Kilwinning, Scotland
1327-1348	Thomas de Rossy	Scottish. Buried Scone, Scotland
1348-1374	William Russell	Manxman. Abbot of Rushen Abbey. Died at Ramshead, England. Buried Furness Abbey
1374-?1381	John Donkan	Manxman. Translated to Derry and then, in 1394, to Down.
1381-1387	Robert Waldby	Translated to Aire in France, and then, in 1391, to Dublin
1387-1392	Possibly vacant	
?1392-1409	John Sprotton	
1410-1429	Richard Payl	Previously Bishop of Dromore. Possibly longer in Mann
1429-1448	Unknown	
1448-1453	John Green	Also Vicar of Dunchurch and Suffragan Bishop of Lichfield
1453-1455	Vacant	
1455-1458	Thomas Burton	Franciscan
1458-1480	Thomas of Kirkham	Abbot of Vale Royal, Cheshire
1480-1486	Richard Oldham	Formerly Abbot of St Werburgh, Chester
1487- c.1521	Huan Hesketh	
1523- c.1540	John Howden	
1545-1548	Robert Ferrar	Translated to St Davids, Wales. Martyred 1555.
1548-1558	Henry Mann	Dean of Chester
1558-1568	Thomas Stanley	Probably the illegitimate second cousin of the 3rd Earl of Derby. Noted pluralist
1569-1573	John Salisbury	The last abbot of Titchfield Abbey. Held deanery of Norwich concurrently with title of Bishop
1573-1576	James Stanley	
1576-1599	John Meyrick	Previously vicar of Hornchurch
1599-1604	George Lloyd	Translated to Chester

1604-1633	John Phillips	Archdeacon of Mann since 1587. Also Archdeacon of Cleveland 1601-1619. Translated the Book of Common Prayer and Bible into Manx
1634-1635	William Forster	Possible Prebendary of Chester
1635-1643	Richard Parr	
1643-1661	Vacant	Commonwealth; puritans do not recognise bishops
1661-1662/3	Samuel Rutter	Archdeacon of Mann from 1640; may have been acting as bishop after the death of Richard Parr
1663-1671	Isaac Barrow	Translated to St Asaph in North Wales
1671-1682	Henry Bridgeman	Also Dean of Chester
1682-1684	John Lake	Formerly Archdeacon of Cleveland. Translated to Bristol and shortly afterwards to Chichester
1685-1692	Baptist Levinz	Became Prebendary of Winchester
1693-1697	Vacant	
1698-1755	Thomas Wilson	Had been personal chaplain to 9th Earl of Derby and tutor to his son. Declined preferment to the much wealthier See of Exeter
1755-1772	Mark Hildesley	Previously Rector of Hitchin. Oversaw translation of Bible into Manx
1773-1780	Richard Richmond	Formerly Chaplain to the 3rd Duke of Atholl. Nominated by Charlotte Murray, the Duchess
1780-1783	George Mason	Nominated by Charlotte Murray now Dowager Duchess
1784-1813	Claudius Crigan	Formerly Rector of St Anne's, Liverpool. Nominated by Charlotte Murray, Dowager Duchess
1814-1827	George Murray	Nephew to 4th Duke of Atholl, Translated to Rochester
1828-1838	William Ward	Concurrently Rector of Great Horkesley, Essex. Defended See against merger with Carlisle
1838-1840	James Bowstead	Fellow of Corpus Christi College. Translated to Lichfield
1840-1841	Henry Pepys	Prebendary of Wells. Translated to Worcester
1841-1846	Thomas Short	Tutor at Christ Church, Oxford. Translated to St Asaph which he had administered for some years as its bishop was ill
1847	Walter Shirley	Rector of the family livings of Shirley and Brailsford and Archdeacon of Derby. Died of pneumonia after a wet journey to Mann. Reigned only two months and nineteen days
1847-1854	Robert Eden	3rd Lord Auckland. Formerly Chaplain to Queen Victoria. Translated to Bath & Wells
1854-1877	Horatio Powys	Formerly Rector and Rural Dean of Warrington
1877-1887	Rowley Hill	Formerly Rector and Rural Dean of Sheffield. Proposed merging See with Liverpool
1887-1892	John Bardsley	Numerous previous church appointments. Translated to Carlisle
1892-1907	Norman Straton	Formerly Archdeacon of Wakefield. Translated to Newcastle
1907-1911	Thomas Drury	Manxman. Had held various church posts on Mann and been Mathematics master at King William's College. Principal of Ridley Hall, Cambridge. Translated to Ripon
1911-1925	James Denton Thompson	Formerly Vicar of Birmingham
1925-1928	Charles Thornton-Duesbury	Manxman. Formerly Rector of Holy Trinity, Marylebone
1928-1943	William Jones	Formerly Archdeacon of Bradford
1943-1954	John Strickland Taylor	Formerly Principal of Wycliffe Hall, Oxford
1954-1966	Benjamin Pollard	Formerly Bishop of Lancaster
1966-1974	(George) Eric Gordon	Formerly Rector of Chelmsford and Provost of Chelmsford Cathedral
1974-1983	Vernon Nicholls	Formerly Archdeacon of Birmingham. Sold Bishopscourt
1983-1989	Arthur Attwell	Formerly Rector of St Michael's, Workington
1989-2003	Noel Jones	Formerly Archdeacon for the Royal Navy and Chaplain for the Fleet
2003-2007	Graham Knowles	Formerly Dean of Carlisle. Became Dean of St Paul's Cathedral
2008-	Robert Paterson	Formerly Canon of the Province of Wales, and Chaplain and Researcher to the Archbishop of York

Although not strictly relevant to a book about the history of the Isle of Man, many readers may be interested to learn a little more about a ceremony which has not changed in essence for hundreds of years. The following, although far from comprehensive, provides a brief summary.

The Tynwald ceremony is held at St John's each year on 5 July, or on 6 July if the fifth is a Sunday. It starts with a service held in the Royal Chapel of St John's and conducted in a mix of English and Manx. Dignitaries then proceed to Tynwald Hill along the processional way which is strewn with marram grass, the local name for which is 'bent'. All those taking part in the Tynwald Day Ceremony also wear a sprig of mugwort (see chapter 9).

Two processions leave the church largely in reverse order of seniority. Tynwald Hill has four tiers and the first procession is made up of those seated on the lowest two. The second procession, often called the Tynwald Court Procession, consists of those seated on the top two tiers of Tynwald Hill. The Manx National Standard precedes the President of Tynwald and the Sword of State precedes the Lord of Mann or his/her representative which is usually the Lieutenant Governor.

Before they reach the war memorial, about half way down the processional way on the north side, the two processions halt and face inwards. The Lord of Man passes between the two lines and the processions reform behind him, effectively turning themselves inside out so that the Lord may be the first to step onto Tynwald Hill.

Seating on Tynwald Hill

Seated on the top tier of Tynwald Hill is the Lord of Man and their consort, or the Lord's representative the Lieutenant Governor and his assistant if necessary. Also seated on the top tier is the President of Tynwald, the Lord Bishop of Sodor & Man, the Members and Clerk of the Legislative Council, the Surgeon to the Household and the Sword Bearer.

On the second tier down is seated the Speaker, Members and Secretary of the House of Keys and their chaplain.

The third tier is occupied by the High Bailiff, the representative of the Commission of the Peace, the Chief Registrar, the Mayor of Douglas, the Chairmen of Commissioners from Castletown, Peel, Ramsey, Laxey, Onchan, Port Erin and Port St Mary, the Archdeacon, the Vicar General, the clergy of various denominations and the Chief Constable.

Seated on the fourth and lowest tier are the four Coroners, Yn Lhaihder (The Reader), and the Captains of the Parish. The fourth tier also carries the two lecterns used by the two deemsters.

Ceremony on Tynwald Hill

One of the coroners and Yn Lhaihder 'fences' the court, the coroner in English and Yn Lhaihder in Manx. Fencing is a proclamation to all those present that no disturbance will be tolerated and that everyone should answer to their names when called. Traditionally no weapons, apart from the Sword of State, were permitted within the symbolic fence.

The four coroners are first sworn in for the next year and receive their staves of office.

The two deemsters then proclaim the laws enacted during the previous year. The First Deemster stands at the lectern on the south side of the hill to promulgate the new laws in English, while the Second Deemster stands at the lectern on the north side to promulgate them in Manx.

The Lord of Man or their representative then invites any members of the public who have a petition for redress of grievance to come forward and hand them to the Clerk of Tynwald who receives them at the foot of the Hill. Such petitions are considered by the Standing Orders Committee of Tynwald at a later date.

At this point the business on the Hill is deemed to have been completed. The processions leave the Hill in the same order and with the same procedure as that used when leaving the church. By this means the Lord, preceded by the Sword of State, is the first to re-enter the church.

Captioning Ceremony

The Court of Tynwald is formed of the President of Tynwald, Legislative Council, Speaker and Members of the House of Keys. Once it has reassembled in the Royal Chapel, the Acts promulgated on Tynwald Hill are captioned. Certificates for each Act are signed first by the Lord of Man or the Lieutenant Governor, then by the President and finally by the Speaker. The Court is then adjourned and the Lord of Man or their representative, the President and Legislative Council retire. The Keys remain to transact any remaining business.

SELECTED BIBLIOGRAPHY

The information for this book has been derived from a number of sources. The author acknowledges with gratitude the debt she owes to the following:

Anon, *Railways in the Isle of Man*, Isle of Man Tourist Board, undated but c. 1968

Anon, *The Old House of Keys*, Manx National Heritage, undated but c. 2002

Basnett, Stan & Pearson, Keith, *Double Century*, Adam Gordon, 1996

Bawden, T.A., Garrad, L.S., Qualtrough, J.K., & Scatchard, J.W., *Industrial Archaeology of The Isle of Man*, David & Charles, 1972

Beckerson, John, *Holiday Isle; the Golden Era of the Manx Boarding House*, The Manx Heritage Foundation, 2007

Beighton, Peter & Douglas, Andrew, *Steve Hislop's 'You couldn't do it Now'*, Mannin Printing Ltd., 1993

Blackburn, C.J., *How the Manx Fleet helped in the Great War*, Louis G. Meyer Ltd, 1923, reprinted for Alastair Lamberton 1993

Broderick, George (translator), *cronica regum mannie & insularum (Chronicles of the Kings of Man and the Isles)*, Manx Museum and National Trust, 1979

Caine, J.B., Cubbon, A.M., Garrad, L.S., Harrison, A.M., Harrison, S., *100 Years of Heritage*, Manx Museum and National Trust, 1994

Chappell, Connery, *Island of Barbed Wire*, Robert Hale, 2005

Chappell, Connery, *The Dumbell Affair*, T. Stephenson & Sons Ltd., 1981

Craine, David, *Manannan's Isle*, Manx Museum and National Trust, 1955

Craine, David, *Tynwald*, The Printing Committee of Tynwald, 1976

Cregeen, Archibald, *A Dictionary of the Manks Language*, Yn cheshaght ghailckagh (The Manx Society), 1969

Cresswell, Yvonne M., *Living with the Wire*, Manx National Heritage, 1994

Cubbon, A.M., *The Ancient & Historic Monuments of the Isle of Man*, Manx National Heritage, 1994

Cubbon, A.M. (ed), *Prehistoric Sites in the Isle of Man*, Manx National Heritage, 1973

Douglas, Mona, *They lived in Ellan Vannin*, Times Press Ltd, 1968

Fargher, Douglas C., *Fargher's English-Manx Dictionary*, Shearwater Press, 1993

Garrad, Larch S., *The Naturalist in the Isle of Man*, David & Charles, 1972

Gelling, Canon John, *A history of the Manx Church 1698-1911*, Manx Heritage Foundation, 1998

Goodwyn, Mike, *Manx Electric*, Platform Five, 1993

Hellowell, John, *A Tour of Manx Lighthouses*, Peter Williams Associates, 1998

Jones, E. Alfred, *The Old Church Plate of the Isle of Man*, Bemrose and Sons, 1907

Kermode, P.M.C., *Manx Crosses*, Bemrose & Sons Ltd., 1907, facsimile edition, Elibron Classics, 2005

Kermode, P.M.C. & Herdman, W.A., *Manks Antiquities*, University Press, Liverpool, 1914

Kinvig, R.H., *The Isle of Man; a social, cultural and political history*, University Press, Liverpool, 1993

Kitto, John, *Historic Homes of the Isle of Man*, Executive Publications, 1990

Kneale, S.J. & Bolton, J.B., *Manx Constitution and Financial Aspects of Isle of Man Government*, Island Development Co. Ltd., 1967

Kniveton, Gordon, *Skianyn Vannin; Wings of Mann*, The Manx Experience, 1997

Laughton, Alfred Nelson, *High-Bailiff Laughton's Reminiscences*, The Manx Experience in conjunction with Dickinson Cruickshank & Co., 1999 (facsimile of text from 1916)

Lewis, Jon E. (ed), *The Mammoth Book of How it Happened*; eye-witness accounts of great historical moments, Robinson, 1998

McDonnell, Hector, *Irish Round Towers*, Wooden Books, 2005

Moore, A.W., *A History of the Isle of Man (2 volumes)*, Manx Museum and National Trust, 1977 (reprint of text from 1900)

Moore, A.W., *The Folk-Lore of the Isle of Man*, Brown & Son, 1891

Moore, A.W. (compiler), *Manx Worthies*, Manx Museum and National Trust, 1971

Morby, John E., *Handbook of Kings & Queens*, Wordsworth, 1994

Morrison, Sophia (ed), *Mannin, a Journal of Matters Past and Present relating to Mann*, Yn cheshaght ghailckagh (The Manx Society), 1913-7

Paton, C.I., *Manx Calendar Customs*, The Folk-Lore Society, 1939

Pearson, Keith, *The Douglas Horse Tramway*, Adam Gordon, 1999

Pickett, Elizabeth, *Isle of Man; foundations of a landscape*, British Geological Survey, 2001

Quilliam, Leslie, *A Gazetteer of the Isle of Man*, Cashtal Books, 2004

Randles, Jenny, *Supernatural Isle of Man*, Robert Hale, 2006

Robinson, David, *The Cistercian Abbeys of Britain*, B.T. Batsford, 2002

Scarffe, Andrew, *The Great Laxey Mine*, Manx Heritage Foundation, 2004

Sargeaunt, B.E., *The Isle of Man and the Great War*, Brown and Sons, 1920

Sargeaunt, B.E., *The Military History of Isle of Man*, T. Buncle & Co. Ltd, 1947

Taylor, Tim, *What Happened When*, Channel 4 Books, 2006

Various, *A Chronicle of the 20th Century Vol I*, The Manx Experience, 1999

Various, *A Chronicle of the 20th Century Vol II*, The Manx Experience, 2000

Various, *Brown's Popular Guide to the Isle of Man*, James Brown & Son, Undated, but c. 1890

Periodicals and papers

Current Archaeology, Number 150. Article on excavation of Billown, Isle of Man by Timothy Darvill of Bournemouth University.

IT Now, January 2010. Announcement that BCS Isle of Man Section had won the President's Challenge 2009.

New Civil Engineer, 26 November 2009. Article on expansion of Isle of Man Airport by Jessica Rowson.

School of Social Science, Liverpool John Moores University, paper entitled 'Shaping the institutions of Manx government: constitutional policy making 1903-2003', by David Kermode

Websites

http://hansard.millbanksystems.com

www.gov.im

www.isle-of-man.com/manxnotebook

INDEX

Page numbers refer only to the most significant references within the text. Pages numbers in *italics* indicate illustrations; italicised pages may also contain relevant text.

Act of Revestment 90-1, 99
Act of Settlement
     see Manx Magna Carta
Albert Tower *114*
Andreas Airfield *122*
Avalonia *5*
Ayres, The *64*, 126, *128*

Baldr 139
Ballachurry Fort
     see Kerroogarroo Fort
Balladoole 32, *33*, 89, 123, 133
Ballafayle Cairn *12*, 13
Ballagawne 16
Ballagilley 85, 103
Ballaglass *8*
Ballakaighan 11, 18
Ballaqueeny 22
Ballateare 33
Ballavarry 12
Bank of Mona *106*, 107, 111
Baronies 41-2, 54-5
Barroose 17
Bellabbey Farm 54
Beltain 23
Bemahague 35, *105*
Bemaken 39
Berrag 19
Bersu, Gerhard 123
Billown 9, 12, 14
Bishopscourt *40*, 41, 82
Bounty 105
Braaid, The 31
Bradda Head 15, 94
Braust 21
Bride 34
Bridge House 95, *96*
Brown, James 104-5
Brown, T.E. 104
Bruce, Alexander 110, 111-2
Buggane 131,137
Bulgham 131, *138*

Cabbals 24
Caledonian Mountain range 5, *9*
Calf of Man 53, 125, *131*
Captain of the Parish 63-64
Cashtal yn Ard *11*, 13
Castle Mona 96, *98*, 128
Castle Rushen 48, *56*, *58*, 59, *67*, 76, *77*, 79-80, 136
Chibbr yn Argid
     see Holy Well of St Patrick

Chibbyr Sheeant
     see Holy Well of St Patrick
Chibbyr Vaghal
     see St Maughold's Well
Cholera *101*
Christian, Edward 74-5
Christian, William
     see Illiam Dhone
Clay Head 18
Close ny Chollagh *16*, 21
Close y Garey 8
Conindrus 23-24
Conister Rocks
     see St Mary's Isle
Council of Ministers 124, 129
Court of Tynwald 129
Cregneash 86, *87*, *124*, *125*, *132*
Crogga House 89, *90*
Cronk Urley 31
Cronkbourne *97*
Crown dependency 128
Culdees 24
Cunningham's Young Men's Holiday Camp *107*, *118*

Deemster 64, 138, 147
Derby, The 73, *74*, *75*
Derby fort *68*, 76
Derbyhaven *66*, 121
Dhoon 114
Douglas Head 36, 108
Douglas Horse Tramway 109, *113*
Douglas Southern Electric Tramway 109-10
Druids 22-3
Dumbell, George William 110-1
Dumbell's Bank 107, 110

Education 84-5, 103-4
Emigration 78, 100-1, 126
Eurasian plate 5
Executive Council
     see Council of Ministers

Fairy Bridge *139*, 140
Fairies 133, 135-6, 141
Falcons *61*, 114
Fargher, Robert 104
Fionn mac Cumhaill 131
First World War 117
Fosterage *20*
Foxdale 93, 141
Futhark *34*

Gaiety Theatre *126*
Giant deer 8
Gilcolm 135
Glen Mooar *22*
Glen Wyllin 31
Godred Crovan 37, 134
Government House
        see Bemahague
Great Laxey Mine 94-5, 111
Great Stanley, The 73-8
Greeba 136
Gretch Veg
        see King Orry's Grave
Groudle 109

Hall Caine, Thomas Henry 116, 121, 136
Hango Hill *81*, 85, 103
Hill forts 19
Hillary, William *102*
Holiday venue 107-10, 113, 117
Holy Well of St Patrick 134
Horse Trams
        see Douglas Horse Tramway
House of Keys *99*, *106*
Howstrake *35*, 108, 109
Human flea 21
Hump-backed scrapers 12

Iapetus ocean 5
Illiam Dhone *79*, 80-2, 83, 138
Industry 88, 93-6
Irish Elk
        see Giant Deer
Irish round tower *36*
Isle of Man Railway Co. 109, 111
Isle of Man Steam Packet Company 113, 118, 122

Jurby 121

Keeill Pheric 134
Keeills 24
Kelly, Harry 87,125
Kermode, Philip 12, 125
Kerroogarroo Fort *76*
Keys, The
        see The Twenty Four
Killeaba 16
King Orry
        see Godred Crovan
King Orry's Grave *135*
King William's College 103-4, 120
Kiondroghad 16
Kirby 83
Kirk Andreas *122*
Kirk Braddan 53
Kirk Malew 79, 135, *137*
Kirk Michael 20, 57, 72
Kitterland *131*, 133

Knockaloe *117*, 118, 122

Lady Isabella *93*, 125
Lag ny Keeilley *23*
Langness *7*, 36, *37*, *86*
Laurentia 5, 15
Legislative Council 119, 129, 147
Loaghtan *10*, 11
Loch, Henry Brougham 105, 107, *109*
Lonan Old Church *24*, *72*
Lorne House 95, *96*

Magnus Barfot 38, 42
Manannan 132
Mannin McLir
        see Manannan
Manx crosses 25, *26*, *34*, *35*, 125
Manx Electric Railway *108*, 109, 113-4, *115*
Manx Gaelic 51, 57, 71, *73*, 92, 125-6
Manx Magna Carta 88
Manx Museum 122, 123, 125
Manx National Anthem 116
Manx Northern Line 109
Manx Post Office 92-3, 127
Marine Drive Tramway
        see Douglas Southern ElectricTramway
Marown Old Church 137
Marram grass 132, 147
Maughold 20, 25, 47, 83, 135, *136*
Meayll Circle *13*, 14, 17
Meayll Hill
        see Mull Hill
Merpeople138
Mona's Isle 21
Monapia 21
Monk's Bridge *55*
Moraine 7
Mugwort 139
Mull Hill 14, 17, 132
Murrey's pence 86

Noble, Henry Bloom 110,112
North Barrule *9*, 132
Nunnery, The 39, *49*

Offshore finance 128
Ogham *25*
Old Grammar School *85*, 125
Onchan 12

Pagan Lady 32
Patrick 38
Peel Castle *59*, *60*
Peggy 94-5, 125
Phynnodderee 136
Point of Ayre 102, *103*
Port Soderick 24, 131
Port-e-Chee 95, *97*

Poyllvaaish 6, *133*

Quakerism
    see Society of Friends
Quarterlands 29

Rectory, Andreas, The 86-7, 122
Romulus 23-4
Ronaldsway 9, 11-2, *48*, 79, *120*, 121
Roolwer 40, *41*
Round houses 17-18
Royal National Lifeboat Institute *102*
Royal Way 50
Runes *34*, *35*
Rushen Abbey 37, 38-40, *52-3*, 53-4, *69*

Samhain 23
Santwat 38, 140
Second World War 121-3, 124
Sheading 38,106
Short Horned Cairn
    see Ballafayle Cairn
Sky Hill *37*, 135
Slieau Whuallian 136
Smelt Monument *100*, 137
Smoke penny 57
Smuggling 74, 88-9, 94-5
Snaefell *9*, 94, 131, 141
Snaefell Mountain Railway 109, 113
Society of Friends 83
Sod hedges 17
Sodor and Man 40-1
Somerled 43, 135
South Barrule *18*, *19*
Speke Farm keeill 24
Spooyt Vane *22*
St Adamnan's Church
    see Lonan Old Church

St Andrew's Church 35
St George's Woollen Mill 97, *98*
St German's Cathedral 41, *42*, 66, *82*
St John's *30*, 139, 147
St Mary's Isle 102-3
St Maughold *134*, 135
St Maughold's Well *134*
St Michael's island 47, *48*, 76
St Patrick 133, *134*
St Patrick's Isle 21, 27, 32, 36, 38
St Runius's Church
    see Marown Old Church
St Trinian's Church *137*
Sword of State 47, 62, 147

Themselves
    see fairies
Things 29-31, 37
Tholt-y-Will 136
Thorwald cross *35*
Three Legs of Mann 46, *47*, 132
Time Team 24
Tourist Trophy (TT) 115-6, 121, 129
Tower of Refuge *102*, 103
Treens 29
Tromode Sailcloth Works 96
Twenty Four, The 63, 75, 97-9, 104-7, 119, 129, 147
Tynwald Hill 17, *29*, *30*, 62, 115, 124, 138, 147

Upper Douglas Cable Tramway *110*, 114

Watch and ward *63*, 75
West Baldwin Reservoir 30
Wilson, Bishop 87, 88
Witches Mill *140*

Yarding 65

POSTSCRIPT

The Isle of Man, Devon, England. This land on the floodplain between the rivers Yarty and Axe is common to the neighbouring parishes of Axminster and Kilmington. It is called the Isle of Man. Why? The author has no idea!